LEROY COLLINS LEON COUNTY PUBLIC LIBRARY

3 1260 01036 5081

DATE DUE

D1435828

FOR THE SAKE OF PEACE

FOR THE
SAKE OF
PEACE

SEVEN PATHS TO
GLOBAL HARMONY

A BUDDHIST PERSPECTIVE

MIDDLEWAY
PRESS

DAISAKU IKEDA

Published by Middleway Press
A division of the SGI-USA
606 Wilshire Blvd., Santa Monica, CA 90401

© 2001 Soka Gakkai

ISBN 0-9674697-2-4

All rights reserved
Printed in the United States of America

10   9   8   7   6   5   4   3   2   1

Cover and interior design by Gopa and the Bear

Library of Congress Cataloging-in-Publication Data

Ikeda, Daisaku.
    For the sake of peace : seven paths to global
harmony, a Buddhist perspective / Daisaku Ikeda.
        p. cm.
Includes bibliographical references and index.
    ISBN 0-9674697-2-4 (hardcover : alk. paper)
1. Peace—Religious aspects—Buddhism.
2. Sōka Gakkai—Doctrines.
3. Buddhism—Social aspects. 4. Buddhism and
humanism. I. Title.
    BQ4570.P4 I36 20001
    294.3'37873—dc21   00-012295

294.3 Ike
01036 5081 05/31/01   LCL
Ikeda, Daisaku.

For the sake of peace :
seven paths to global
                      AP

LeRoy Collins
Leon County Public Library
200 W. Park Avenue
Tallahassee, FL 32301

CONTENTS

Since wars begin in the minds of men,
it is in the minds of men that the
defenses of peace must be constructed.

From the Preamble of the UNESCO Constitution

FOREWORD

READERS OF THIS BOOK from whatever faith or perspective
will be rewarded by an opportunity to engage in a "dialogue"
with the thoughts of one of the twenty-first century's foremost peace leaders. In this "dialogue," readers can bring to
bear their own life experiences, knowledge and aspirations.
It is difficult to imagine readers whose inner strength, global
vision and spirit of inquiry will not benefit from engagement
in this process.

I first met the author, Daisaku Ikeda, president of the Soka
Gakkai International, in Tokyo in December 1980. The meeting had been arranged through the kind introduction of the
late internationally respected Professor Hiroharu Seki, professor emeritus of Tokyo University, a uniquely creative
peace studies pioneer, then director of the Institute of Peace
Science at Hiroshima University.

My "dialogue" with President Ikeda had begun even
before this first meeting. It began by reading a small paperback book *Toward the 21st Century: Addresses by Daisaku Ikeda*

(1978), compiled by students of the Soka University International Student Center. It contained talks to students and others between 1968 and 1977 related to the founding of Soka University. These talks evidenced the wisdom of a great humanist educator dedicated to nurturing youthful intellect for lifelong creative contributions to the well-being of humanity.

While observing that the great private universities of the world originally had been created on spiritual foundations, he cautioned that they could not have become great if dominated by religious dogmas. He declared that a truly great university must be dedicated to "the emancipation of the human spirit." Therefore he called upon the students to "Be creative individuals!" He invited the students to join as co-founders of a value-creating university devoted to "intellectual excellence and world peace for the benefit of all mankind." Reminding all of the "sanctity of life," he donated a bronze statue bearing the words: "For what purpose should one cultivate wisdom? May you always ask this question!"

As a scholar educated in four private institutions with religious roots that had developed traditions of excellence and service—Phillips Exeter Academy, Princeton University, Harvard University and Northwestern University—I was struck by Soka University's principles of independence and intellectual freedom in my first "dialogue" with its founder. In addition, as a Korean War veteran become political scientist and scientific apologist for war [*The Korean Decision: June*

24–30, 1950 (1968)], and as a scholar only belatedly awakened during 1973–74 to the spirit of "No more killing!"—
I was especially inspired by President Ikeda's vision of an
entire university dedicated to peace. This is expressed in the
last of Soka University's three founding mottoes: "Be a
fortress of peace for all mankind!"

Thus through this "dialogue" I was able to add the peace
spirit of Soka University to the nonviolent spirit of Gandhigram Rural University in Tamil Nadu, India, founded by the
late great Gandhian educator Dr. G. Ramachandran. For
three weeks in 1976, under Dr. Ramachandran's tutelage and
that of Professor N. Radhakrishnan, I had been privileged to
study Gandhigram's total commitment to nonviolent service
and its unique Shanti Sena (Peace Force) as an alternative to
military training.

Against this background of "dialogue" mediated by reading, when I first met President Ikeda on December 18, 1980,
our dialogue centered on the importance of creativity in
realizing global conditions of principled respect for life. He
said that he greatly respected creative thinking and that the
importance of this had been emphasized by his revered mentor, Josei Toda. For my part, I replied that I most admired
the ability to translate creative ideas into action. I recalled
that once when teaching politics at Princeton I had asked
Governor Muñoz-Marin of Puerto Rico, who was a poet as
well as politician, what the similarities and differences were
between these two roles. He replied: "Both the poet and the

political leader have the creative ability to imagine non-exist-
ing states of affairs. But the political leader has the additional
ability to influence other people to bring them about."

Daisaku Ikeda also combines the talents of poetry and
leadership. A poet, writer and photographer, he celebrates
the literary, visual and performing arts of every culture.
Effectively evoking the cooperation of others, he is an inex-
haustible builder of institutions. Among them are local and
national lay Buddhist organizations for mutual support and
service, educational institutions from kindergartens to two
universities, a multimillion circulation newspaper, a publishing house, an art museum, a concert association, cultural
centers, a research center, a global policy institute and, early
in his work, even a democratic political party.

Since 1960, he has been a tireless global peace educator
—encouraging local membership groups, engaging in peace
dialogues with world leaders and cultural figures, lecturing
at universities and establishing cultural exchange networks of
mutual respect. Courageously and effectively he has crossed
Cold War boundaries to pioneer in establishing peaceful cultural relations with antagonists on both sides such as with
Russia and China, the United States and Europe.

For his efforts he has been showered with honors from
throughout the world. These include peace awards, literary
awards, honorary degrees, honorary citizenships and, most
important, affection from a vast number of people who have
been uplifted through his guidance in practical application

of humanist Buddhist principles in daily life. Like all major peace figures in history he has encountered opposition as well as received support. The path to peace has not been and will not be easy. But as he advises, "Never be defeated!"

The remarkable result of such leadership has been to facilitate the emergence of a worldwide humanist Buddhist movement for peace, culture and education that now embraces some twelve million people in 163 countries — the Soka Gakkai International, which has been an outstandingly constructive supporter of the humanitarian and peace programs of the United Nations.

In *For the Sake of Peace*, Daisaku Ikeda invites us to a "dialogue" on seven paths to peace that seek to overcome major obstacles to global well-being. The courage, clarity and informed nature of his call to follow "The Path of Disarmament" contrasts greatly with the silence or contrary advocacy by political leaders of today's major military states. For this alone respectful readers may wish to award him a people's peace prize for the twenty-first century.

Glenn D. Paige
Center for Global Nonviolence, Honolulu

PREFACE

IN 1937, I was nine years old. It seemed my father was finally beginning to recover from a long illness. It was then that my eldest brother, Kiichi, was drafted into the army. He was twenty-one. He was very earnest and sincere, and I respected him a lot.

While our father was ill, Kiichi had worked hard to support us, becoming the pillar and mainstay of our family. First he and then my three other elder brothers—all in the prime of life—were snatched away from us by the military. As a result, the responsibility to care for our aged parents fell to me, weak and sick with tuberculosis. My father's illness also persisted. What cruel demands nationalism makes on the lives of ordinary people!

In the early spring of 1939, two years after he had been drafted, Kiichi was sent abroad to fight. We received notification from the army that we could go to see him before he was shipped overseas, so my mother and I hurried to Tokyo

Station. I was a fifth grader by then. My mother prepared some food, mainly rice balls—a veritable feast in wartime Japan—which she generously wrapped in large sheets of seaweed. As she said, "We won't be seeing him for a long time."

When we got to the station, there were about three hundred soldiers on their way to the front. Their families had gathered with them in the open area in front of the station. Since the young men were headed for the battle front, this might well be their final farewell. The eyes of many mothers and young wives were filled with tears.

The soldiers' departure was so sudden that the families of those from regions far away from Tokyo, such as Yamagata and Akita, did not have time to get to Tokyo to say goodbye. I still have a clear memory of those soldiers sitting quietly in their uniforms on the sidewalk outside the station with no one to talk to, their shoulders drooping. My mother called out to several of them to join us, and she sent me to hand rice balls to those who seemed too shy to accept her invitation. Their forlorn expressions brightened, and they smiled and talked as they shared in the humble yet heartfelt repast my mother had made.

Finally, though it broke our hearts, the time for departure arrived. My brother retied his gaiters, checked the sword in his belt and returned to his squad.

My mother and I headed back by public railway to Shinagawa Station on our way home. We were waiting on the platform in the hope that my brother's train would pass through the station when a train full of soldiers pulled in.

My mother dashed from window to window, looking for my brother, but she was unable to find him. Just then, an elderly station attendant, sympathizing with our plight, grabbed a megaphone and began calling in a loud voice: "Is Kiichi Ikeda there? Is Kiichi Ikeda there? Your mother is here to see you." He walked up and down the platform for us, searching for my brother.

The train was preparing to pull out when one of my brother's comrades heard the attendant's call. I think it was one of the boys who were with us earlier. He rushed to my brother, who was sitting on the other side of the train, and said, "Kiichi, it's your mother!"

The train had quietly started to move. My brother flew to the window and leaned out to see her.

"Kiichi, Kiichi, take care of yourself!" my mother called as she chased after the accelerating train for several steps. My brother nodded silently and waved his arm vigorously.

My mother and I continued to wave goodbye until the train had completely disappeared from sight.

In 1941, Kiichi was temporarily discharged and came back to us from China. It was at this time that he said to me, his voice shaking with anger, "The Japanese army is too cruel for words."

Four years later later, Kiichi fell victim to the ill-fated Imphal Campaign. He died in Burma (now Myanmar) in January 1945. He was twenty-nine.

I am against war! I am absolutely opposed to it! Many young men of my generation were incited by the military government to go proudly to the battle front and give their lives there. The families left behind were praised for their sacrifices as "military mothers" and "families of soldiers at the front"—terms deemed to carry high honor.

But in reality, what agony and grief swirled in the depths of their hearts! What deep wounds did the contrived praises and sympathy of others, oblivious to this inner turmoil, inflict on the aching hearts of the mothers and children left behind!

A mother's love, a mother's wisdom, is too great to be fooled by such false phrases as "for the sake of the nation." In May 1945, when I was seventeen, a youthful American pilot parachuted down near the place to which my family had evacuated. He had been flying a B-29 bomber that was downed in a fierce night battle. This young man was hit and kicked brutally and repeatedly by those who happened to be where he landed. Eventually, blindfolded, he was taken off to prison by military police. When I reported to my mother how this soldier had been attacked, she said: "What a pity! I'm sure his mother is very concerned about him." My mother's utterance is still deeply etched in my memory.

During the war, every season of the year was like winter. Then, finally, when the war ended, a new sun of peace began to rise on the horizon—quiet, yet shining bright and strong.

I heard the emperor's August 15, 1945, radio announce-
ment of the end of the war. My complex feelings at that time
remain indelibly engraved in the core of my being.

I am absolutely opposed to war. That is one reason why I
so highly respect Tsunesaburo Makiguchi and Josei Toda,
who, imprisoned by the military government, became foremost champions of truth and justice.

I am determined to fight against anyone who supports or
advocates war. I will fight the dark, demonic forces of
destruction! And I am joined by an impressive force of close
to twelve million people who, armed with brilliant strength
of spirit, are powerfully committed to the cause of genuine
lasting peace.

Since 1983, the year the Soka Gakkai International—the
organization of which I am president—was accredited as a
nongovernmental organization (NGO) of the United
Nations, I have been issuing an annual peace proposal to the
heads of various governments, other NGOs, academic institutions, libraries and U.N. officials. Each proposal contains
observations on the state of the world, analyses of the underlying philosophical issues that must be dealt with if we are
to achieve peace, as well as suggestions for concrete actions
that can be taken. *For the Sake of Peace* is a most valuable
opportunity to share many of my thoughts with a wider
audience—especially the youth around the globe, who are
our future—with the hope and conviction that as citizens of

the world, we can discover our common humanity. That, of course, is the basis for all efforts for peace. I deeply appreciate the efforts of the staff of Middleway Press, who conceived of this project to which I readily agreed, and to the editors who have helped me arrange my ideas into the thematic chapters you'll find in the pages to come. I also offer my sincere thanks to Glenn D. Paige for his kind words and invaluable contribution to this project.

Above all, we cannot let the tragedy we have experienced be repeated by generations to come. We must create a path to peace and friendship for youth and for the twenty-first century.

Daisaku Ikeda

chapter 1

THE PROSPECT

OF PEACE

THE PROSPECT
OF PEACE

WHEN THE TWENTIETH CENTURY BEGAN, there was a general belief that human progress was limitless. The lofty ideals and high purposes envisioned at the outset of the century were obliterated, however, by the extremist ideologies that swept the world, leaving slaughter in their wake. Perhaps no other century has been witness to such endless tragedy and human folly; the global environment has been grievously damaged, and the gap between rich and poor seems ever widening.

The last years of the century proved to be a period of dramatic transformations. It seemed, at first, that the end of the Cold War in 1989 heralded far brighter prospects for humanity's future, but those hopes were soon dashed as the world was wracked by regional and internal conflicts. It was as if the Iron Curtain had been finally pried open only to unleash the pent-up demonic forces of war and violence. Since then, more than fifty nations have undergone the wrenching drama of violent conflict, division or independence. These wars have claimed millions of lives.

Humankind is faced on every side by inescapable dilemmas: the threat of nuclear arms and other weapons of mass destruction, the intensification of ethnic discord, damage to the environment from the effects of global warming and destruction to the earth's ozone layer, and the spread of psychopathic, brutal criminality.

Now we stand at the start of the third millennium. At this moment in history, we should determine to eliminate all needless suffering from this planet that is our home. In our efforts to realize this goal, we will find the key to ensuring that the new century does not mimic the last but begins an era of peace and hope. Now is the time to build a new age that shines with the glory of humanity and culture by focusing again on the sanctity of life.

We are charged with the task of achieving not just a passive peace—the absence of war—but of transforming those social structures that threaten human dignity in order to realize the positive, active values of peace. Efforts to enhance international cooperation and the fabric of international law are, of course, also necessary. But more vital are the creative efforts of individuals to develop a culture of peace, because it is on this foundation that a new global society can be built.

What Is the Path to Peace?

What is needed to advance human history, to move from darkness to light, from despair to hope, from killing to coexistence? What light can dispel the gloom and illuminate the expanses of the next thousand years? These are questions we must ask ourselves in all earnestness.

Josei Toda, my mentor and the second president of the Soka Gakkai, passionately longed to eliminate misery from the face of the earth. His fervent wish forms the basis of my thought and action. During the crucial middle part of the twentieth century, Mr. Toda advocated a Buddhist humanism and instituted actions designed to stem the flow of human unhappiness. He insisted that all our notions of progress must take into account forecasts of conditions two hundred years in the future. At the same time, he exhorted us to use dialogue as a way to create an enduring solidarity that embraces all of humankind.

My own efforts to discuss the most vital topics with informed and concerned people from all over the world are my response to Mr. Toda's exhortation. I am convinced that in plotting a course for the twenty-first century we must both learn lessons from the present and uncover spiritual treasures from the subterranean currents of history. To accomplish this, I have entered into dialogue with representatives of all peoples on the basis of our common humanity.

Barriers to Peace

The first question that arises when one takes on a task so clearly and absolutely positive is this: What inhibits the world from making peace? It is important to know where our resistance lies.

Isolationism

The first obstacle is intrinsic to the scale of the undertaking, which can be overwhelming for people lacking a solid, inclusive spiritual foundation. The former U.N. secretary-general, Boutros Boutros-Ghali, when we met in July 1998, summarized the spiritual landscape of humanity at the end of the century: In light of the globalization of financial, environmental and health issues, domestic problems cannot be solved without addressing international ones. People must be interested, he said, not only in their own countries but also in international conditions. They feel uneasy, however, when confronted with the tide of internationalization and withdraw into their own small "village" (region or state) and traditions, tending to avoid encounters with foreigners. He called this a "new isolationism."

The Illusion of "Efficiency"

A second barrier to break through is another form of self-limitation, in this case resulting from the supremacy of technology. Undeniably, the twentieth century has benefited us greatly in the form of the many advantages of techno-scientific progress. In some instances, however, disregarding humanity, "progress" has proceeded down an arbitrary path with frequently tragic consequences. The crux of this is the principle of efficiency that has come to rule people's think-ing in the modern world. Efficiency advocates stress the most effective, the most efficient and the most convenient. The pursuit of efficiency has stimulated scientific and materialis-tic advances, but its insidious tendency to reduce human beings to mere things is often overlooked. For instance, at the height of the debate on nuclear deterrence there was much talk of assured destruction, damage limitation, cost-versus-benefit ratio and other similar terms. Such merciless and grotesque language derives from the cult of efficiency, which relegates human beings to the status of things and pur-sues expediency at the expense of countless human lives. Politicians and scientists — the elite of the nuclear civiliza-tion and establishment — succumb most easily to the doc-trine of efficiency. This sacrifice to the god of efficiency has cast a shadow over all arms-reduction talks.

A sternly critical examination of the extent to which so-called progress has actually contributed to human happiness must form a large part of our efforts to pioneer a path of hope in the twenty-first century. My actions are founded on the belief that this is humankind's great responsibility.

Greed

A third obstacle to peace is rooted in the fundamental moti-vation of greed for power. The twentieth century began in the midst of vicious power clashes for domination and colo-nial expansion among the great powers. In *A Geography of*

Human Life, Tsunesaburo Makiguchi, the first president of the Soka Gakkai, described these competing powers as glowering at one another, ready unashamedly and cruelly to snatch up other people's land at the slightest opportunity.[1] Their struggle for dominance spawned not only two world wars but also the Cold War, which spread the threat of nuclear confrontation over the whole world.

Owing to the frantic Cold War arms race between Eastern and Western blocs, military might escalated beyond human control. Arms intended to annihilate an enemy menaced the survival of their possessors and drove humanity to the brink of global destruction. Human destiny hung in a perilous balance.

Though Cold War walls have now tumbled, the struggle for supremacy still rages, albeit in a different mode. The drive for global unification through military might has given way to a new struggle for economic domination, under the banner of open markets and free competition where the law of the jungle pervades. In what has been called the "casino" of global capital markets, huge sums of money surpassing the scale of the real economy change hands every day. All this takes place beyond the regulatory reach of national governments and under the slogan of market principles.

Poverty
If the grip of such ingrained greed seems difficult to loosen, a fourth obstacle is even more primal: *need*. In many cases, the causes of the devastating conflicts in various parts of the

world are rooted in economic deprivation. The central issue of the current era is crushing poverty. There can be no peace where hunger reigns.

We must eradicate hunger and poverty and devote attention to establishing a system of economic welfare for the approximately five hundred million people who suffer from malnutrition today and to the two-thirds of the world's nations that are impoverished.

Instead of engaging in cutthroat competition, we should strive to create value. In economic terms, this means a transition from a consumer economy—the mad rush for ownership and consumption—to a constructive economy where all human beings can participate in the act of creating lasting worth.

Environmental Irresponsibility

A fifth obstacle to peace impacts not only human civilizations but all life on the planet: disregard of the environment. Economic growth and prosperity brought about by technological advancement have so captured people's imaginations that the progress and spread of the civilization of science and technology has known no limits and no barriers.

But now we find the triumph to be marred, with damage to the earth's environment inflicted by the side effects of that civilization, telling us that progress may in fact turn out to be our downfall. Air, water and soil pollution, indiscriminate cutting of vast forests, desertification, damage to the earth's protective ozone layer and the resultant effects of global warming: none of these issues can be simply left to resolve themselves. Today, ecologists are telling us that if radical changes are not made, life as we know it might not survive another century.

It has become clear that the solution to such global issues as environmental destruction will require new approaches that transcend national boundaries. Action to assure the survival of humanity cannot be taken as long as our thinking is bound in the narrow confines of the sovereign state. A way of thinking that is rooted in a truly global outlook is the most pressing need of our times.

Nuclear Negativity

The final obstacle humankind must contend with is the ultimate embodiment of human negativity: nuclear weapons.

Nuclear security and nuclear equilibrium are essentially impossible to achieve. Buddhism teaches the oneness of life and its environment, which means that the subjective world is inseparably linked to the objective world. Because of this bond, as long as the objective environment includes the threat of nuclear weapons, humanity can know no peace.

Preparing for Peace

Depending on one's point of view, these barriers may seem monumental if not eternally immovable. A closer look at the

world today, however, will reveal a number of causes for optimism about humankind's capacity for change: the rise of the
"soft power" of knowledge and expertise in place of the "hard
power" of military might, political authority and wealth; a
growing commitment to nonviolent transfer of power, as
witnessed in the forging of the "rainbow nation" of former
president Nelson Mandela's South Africa; the flourishing of
"people power," reflected in the upsurge of an estimated ten
thousand non-governmental organizations addressing human
rights and safety issues; and the miraculous dissolution of
Bolshevism, which from its very birth was marked by violence and terrorism, without a bloody holocaust.

What can we learn from these positive outcomes that can
be applied elsewhere to pacify the world's current clashes
and avoid a violent future? We may talk of a third millennium, but the mere change in calendar dates will not bring
about a change in the nature of the age. Only human will
and action can create history and open new horizons.

Not long ago I met with Austrian Chancellor Franz Vran-
itzky in Tokyo. He said to me then: "There is an old Latin
proverb that goes 'If you desire peace, prepare for war,' but
in my mind, the saying should be 'If you desire peace, prepare
for peace.' And that is what guides me in my work."

But how do we prepare for peace? Which paths will lead
us out of our internal wildernesses and allow us to live
together happily, the way humanity has always dreamed of?

Paths to Peace

The first path is taken alone: Whether we can become good citizens of the world hinges upon the degree of self-control we can achieve. The ability to see ourselves penetratingly enables us to transcend national boundaries and ethnic lines.

Self-restraint is a prerequisite of the second stage of the journey: the path of dialogue. I cannot emphasize enough its importance, because I believe that the propensity for logic and discussion is the proof of one's humanity. In other words, only when we are immersed in an ocean of language do we become truly human. In *Phaedo,* Plato astutely associates hatred of language (*mislogos*) with hatred of people (*misanthropos*). To abandon dialogue is in fact to abandon being human; and if we abandon our humanity, we cease to be the agency of history, relinquishing this authority to something of a lower order, a kind of bestiality. We know only too well that history is filled with tragedies where bestiality, in the name of ideology or dogma, trampled upon humankind with brutal force and violence.

Dialogue — an open, respectful connection among people — will serve people best if they share a common vision free of illusions; without it, the path of dialogue has a shaky foundation. Underlying the fanfare announcing the new age is a deafening, frightening roar, produced as the familiar systems making up our world order are torn down forever. To overcome the identity crises undermining the soul of modern humanity, we must attempt to discover a new sense of community based on a new cosmology.

Unless that cosmology is to remain in the realm of abstract ideas, it must be translated into the fabric of life: To lay the foundations for a lasting peace, we must deinstitutionalize war. We must effect a transition from a culture of war to a culture of peace. It is time to formulate a set of clear, basic principles on which to build a culture of peace. I am confident that if people everywhere engage in sincere dialogue to identify a common basis for belief and action, and if all people join as equal partners to create that culture of peace, we will witness the dawn of an era in which happiness can be enjoyed by everyone.

Culture defines communities, but larger entities are already in place that exert powerful influences on the world: The role of nations, too, must be transformed. However halting our progress toward a world less centered on nation-states may be, what is entirely clear is that a world in which states count for less is a world in which individual people will count for more.

As the role and responsibility of individuals shaping history grow, it becomes all the more critical that we each learn to live as creative and active global citizens, recognizing and working to fulfill our respective responsibilities in the new millennium.

Finally, at the convergence of the paths is a process that will not be difficult after the rigors of the journey: total disarmament.

War Normalizes Insanity

As a Buddhist following the philosophy of the thirteenth-century Japanese teacher Nichiren and the example set by Josei Toda, I deeply believe that no individual can experience true happiness or tranquility until we turn humankind away from its obsession with war. War has held humankind in its irrevocable grip throughout history; it is the source of all evil. War normalizes insanity — the kind that does not hesitate to destroy human beings like so many insects and tears all that is human and humane to shreds, producing an unending stream of refugees. It also cruelly damages our natural environment.

We have already paid a heavy price for the lesson that nothing is more tragic and cruel than war. I believe we have as our first priority an obligation to our children to open a clear and reliable path to peace in the twenty-first century.

2
chapter

THE PATH OF

SELF-MASTERY

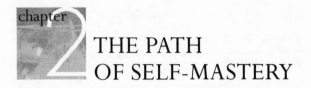

chapter

2 THE PATH
OF SELF-MASTERY

PEACE CANNOT BE A MERE STILLNESS, a quiet interlude between wars. It must be a vital and energetic arena of life-activity, won through our own volitional, proactive efforts. Peace must be a living drama — in Spinoza's words, "a virtue that springs from force of character."[1] Eternal peace is a continuum consciously maintained through the interaction of self-restraining individuals within a self-restraining society.

No one will argue with this description of harmony. Its opposite arises when we strive ruthlessly to attain apparently conflicting aims, often driven by the "no justice–no peace" ethic that propelled revolutionaries of every creed during the twentieth century. In that context, self-restraint is not valued. But as we shall see, *especially* within such conflicts, self-restraint is essential, self-restraint that comes from introspection.

The ability to perceive the negative in oneself enables one to perceive the positive in others. As in relations between individuals, relations between countries cannot be managed on a mature level if one side insists on its own point of view without regard for the position of the other side. I do not mean to advocate a Manichaean concept of the duality of good and evil but only to emphasize that we must acknowledge the good and evil within each of us. Even as we lock horns with a rival, we should be seeking to manifest the good and obliterate the bad. The power of self-restraint can help us avoid conflict and estrangement and enable us to take a correct stance of mutual acceptance and respect.

The Fallacy of Relying on External Reform

The external approach to social change was declared suspect some sixty years ago when, alarmed by the advancing threat of fascism to humanist and democratic values, the British poet T. S. Eliot made a ringing appeal on radio. He said, in part:

> One reason why the lot of the secular reformer or revolutionist seems to me to be the easier is this: that for the most part he conceives of the evils of the world as something external to himself. They are thought of either as completely impersonal, so that there is nothing to alter but machinery; or if there is evil incarnate, it is always incarnate in the other people—a class, a race, the politicians, the bankers, the armament makers, and so forth— never in oneself.

Eliot makes a very basic point that has been well illustrated in the domino-like ripplings of change throughout Eastern Europe. Communist regimes toppled because for too long they sought enemies outside of themselves, not attempting to see the evils they harbored within. And so the view of history as one of class struggle — that is, if class distinctions were obliterated, all social evils would be obliterated — has been bankrupted. Replacing "class" with "race," you have the diabolic Nazi myth that only the Aryan race was pure enough to rule. The myth dies hard. Even today, more than fifty years after World War II, ongoing ultrarightist resistance to the entry of foreign workers into Western European countries is tinged with racist overtones.

Dangers of the "Abstract Spirit"

Even those nineteenth-century revolutions born of "pure" motives — the quest for liberty, equality, fraternity — fell prey to what the great French thinker Gabriel Marcel calls the "abstract spirit." A vivid illustration of its insidious effects can be found in Anatole France's novel *Les Dieux Ont Soif* (The Gods Are Thirsty). Like many revolutionaries, Gamelin, the hero, was not born a cold-blooded human being. Quite the contrary, he was a gentle and compassionate young man, who, despite being severely hungry, calmly shared his meager bread with a starving mother and child. He was pure and giving, ready to sacrifice himself without a trace of regret. The frightening thing is that the purer and more idealistic a young person is, the more susceptible he tends to be to the spell of the "abstract spirit." Before long, appointed juror to the Revolutionary Tribunal and burning with revolutionary zeal, he passes his harsh judgments, putting aside all his personal feelings, and sends many of his enemies to the guillotine. But his own turn comes, and eventually he himself is beheaded, along with his mentor, Robespierre.

In a way, it is easy to revise the laws and reconstruct the system in such a way as to bid farewell to the *ancien régime*. But it is a far different matter to attempt the reconstruction of human beings. To put it in plain language, in human affairs you cannot push things too far too quickly. To rush matters is to force them on people through violence and threats. We see this with political radicalism, which is virtually always shadowed by violence.

The theme was repeated with the Bolsheviks. Certainly, it seems impossible to doubt their sincerity. In fact, Lenin's wife, Krupskaya, and other key people involved with educational theory during Bolshevism's early stages were exceedingly well-intentioned optimists who served in the cause of natural education as espoused in Rousseau's *Émile*. But unless people thoroughly confront their own egoism, there's no telling when their simple good intentions will be transformed into a desire to rule, a desire that seeks approval by clothing itself in the fine costume of ideology. It was also the

hidden evil of the "abstract spirit" that angered Dr. Zhivago
in Pasternak's great novel:

> Reshaping me! People who can say that never un-
> derstand a thing about life, they have never felt its
> breath, its heartbeat, however much they have seen
> or done. They look on it as a lump of raw material
> that needs to be processed by them, to be ennobled
> by their touch. But life is never a material, a sub-
> stance to be molded. If you want to know, life is the
> principle of self-renewal, it is constantly renewing
> and remaking and changing and transfiguring itself,
> it is infinitely beyond your or my obtuse theories
> about it.[2]

The primary cause of that hidden evil lies in the tendency
of the "abstract spirit" to attempt to impose order upon the
human spirit from the outside, often by means of external
pressure. Real progress or reform in the human condition
cannot be effected unless it develops spontaneously through
internal urges and internal strength. At most, external forces
are mere secondary factors that serve to arouse the internal
process. Nevertheless, those possessed by the "abstract spirit"
have utterly neglected internal factors as idealistic. They
have gone to the extreme, trying to squeeze everything into
the premolded framework of an external ideology. The land-
slide collapse of socialist society witnessed at the twentieth

century's close is testimony to the bankruptcy of this unreasonable attempt. And the spiritual desolation revealed once the disguise of ideology was torn away has demonstrated with horrible clarity just how cruelly the "abstract spirit" wreaks destruction in the human heart.

Radicalism and Violence

Why does the violence inherent in radicalism so often undercut the humanistic basis of revolution? Mahatma Gandhi and his successor, Jawaharlal Nehru, clearly perceived the evil of the political radicalism that arises from the "abstract spirit." Among Gandhi's famous words are the following:

> This socialism is as pure as crystal. It, therefore, requires crystal-like means to achieve it. Impure means result in an impure end.... Therefore only truthful, nonviolent and pure-hearted socialists will be able to establish a socialist society in India and the world.[3]

This penetrating insight hits directly on the true nature of socialism. To be sure, socialist theory espouses beautiful ideals that have an abstract kind of logical consistency. For that very reason, people urgently press forward to realize those ideals in concrete form. Obviously, if something is known to be good, the faster it is put into practice the better. As a result, people are in too much of a hurry to reform the system, and they tend to neglect human beings, the most important part of the reform process. The fatal flaw of socialism, therefore, lies not in *failed* efforts to nurture the "truthful, nonviolent, and pure-hearted" but rather in the total *absence* of effort to nurture such people.

Inner Reform

Political systems aside, what *can* nurture truthful, nonviolent and pure-hearted people? The building of lasting peace depends on how many people capable of self-restraint can be fostered through religious practice. If a religion is worthy of the name, and if it can respond to the needs of contemporary times, it should nurture in its followers the spiritual base for becoming good citizens of the world.

In Mahayana Buddhism, there are ten potential conditions of life inherent in a human being, known as the Ten Worlds. According to this principle, people who start wars exist in the four lowest states of Hell, Hunger, Animality and Anger, known together as the "four evil paths." Controlled by instinct and desire, their thoughts and actions are inevitably foolish and barbaric. Therefore, from the Buddhist point of view, the issue of how to build, as the UNESCO Constitution says, the "defenses of peace" within the hearts of such individuals takes precedence over any external systemic factors and represents both the wellspring and the core of any attempt to build world peace.

Buddhism emphasizes the importance of the quality of our motivation, valuing that which issues spontaneously from within, as expressed in the simple phrase, "It is the heart that is important."[4]

It teaches that the ultimate objective of the Buddha's life was revealed in the humanity he manifested in his behavior and actions. Thus the cultivation and perfection of a person's character are considered in the Buddhist tradition to be the true goals of religious training. Norms that are not inner-generated and do not encourage the development of individual character are ultimately weak and ineffective. Only when external norms and inner values function in a mutually supportive manner can they enable people to resist evil and live as genuine advocates and champions of human rights.

The Internal Republic

In examining internal and external norms, it may be illuminating here to look back at Plato's ideas on democracy. In the eighth book of *The Republic,* Plato describes five types of government—aristocracy, timocracy, oligarchy, democracy and tyranny. He analyzes each system, ranking them according to their pros and cons, and goes on to describe the types of human nature to which each system is best suited. In Plato's ranking, democracy comes fourth; the system for which he reserves the highest regard is the benevolent aristocracy committed to the love of knowledge.

Plato's low regard for democracy may stem from the fact that he spent his youth in the confused days of the decline of democracy in Athens. The Peloponnesian War between Athens and Sparta began just before Plato was born. When it ended almost thirty years later with the defeat of Athens, Plato was twenty-five or twenty-six. Thus the greater part of his youth was spent among the trials of this interminable war. Soon after its outbreak, Athens lost its great statesman Pericles to disease, and Athenian democracy rapidly deteriorated. An exceptionally sensitive and perceptive young man, Plato saw humanity at its ugliest. His view of his fellow men and of government must necessarily have been colored by what he observed, and it led him to a stern indictment of human egoism and to a critical view of reality.

The final blow for Plato must have been the execution of his beloved teacher, Socrates, by demagogues capable only of catering to a blind and easily agitated populace. As far as Plato was concerned, Socrates had been murdered by Athenian democracy. It had put to death the most righteous person. No wonder he was skeptical of democracy.

The deeply engraved experiences of his youth gave Plato rare insight into the nature of humankind and society. His detailed, at times comical, portrayal of democracy's innate tendency to transform itself into its exact opposite — tyranny — is a persuasive masterpiece of reason.

This brings us to the paradox of freedom. Advocates of democracy, says Plato, argue that freedom is the greatest virtue of democracy and that, therefore, a democracy is the only state suitable to human beings, whose nature is essentially free. Yet by supporting the insatiable pursuit of freedom, democracy nurtures a multitude of desires that gradually and insidiously "seize the citadel of the young man's soul" and lead him down the path of conceit. Modesty is dismissed as silliness, temperance is shamed as unmanly, and moderation and orderly expenditure are called boorish and mean.

Finally, the situation gets out of control and a strong leader is sought to restore order. From among the "idle drones," a single stinger-equipped creature is chosen, who at first emerges as the leader of the masses but who soon gives in to the diabolical lure of power and is inevitably transformed into a tyrant. And so as Plato astutely points out, "The excess of liberty, whether in States or individuals, seems only to pass into excess slavery" in the hands of a dictator.

This summary of Plato's ideas is admittedly a bit simplistic, yet it vividly shows the pathology and the paradox of liberty. Its lure is irresistible, but it is very difficult to cope with; it continues to be a heavy burden to bear. Following the eloquent arguments of *The Republic* today, we are struck by how persuasively and truthfully Plato establishes his case. How faithfully its chapters record the patterns by which even the totalitarian regimes of our present day have come into being.

Plato's strong criticism of democracy has been attacked and refuted by many modernist ideologues who do not take kindly to his contention that women and children should be looked after communally, that the state should be dominated by a small number of philosophers, and that poets should be expelled, denouncing his ideal as an extreme form of communism.

The French philosopher Alain probably comes closest to correctly interpreting Plato's arguments when he asks whether anyone has even attempted to perceive Plato's *Republic* as the individual's guide to inner self-control. Alain sees Plato's opus more as a discourse on human nature than on government, especially in the way it revolves around the concept of the soul. He adds that the parts about government are capricious, saying they are purposely inserted to confuse the hasty reader. Plato would rather not be understood at all than be misunderstood, Alain says.

The Health of the Soul

Plato's pen shifts quickly from a discussion of institutions to the subject of human character. Immediately after his description of the five types of states and the sorts of human character suited to them in the eighth book of *The Republic*, Plato devotes the ninth book to matters of the "health of the soul" and the "harmony of the soul." This is the natural consequence of his main purpose in writing the work. Plato describes the soul as comprising three parts, the rational, the irascible and the concupiscent, and concludes that the health and harmony of the soul are realized only when the rational part governs and the irascible part obeys. By the end of the ninth book, it is obvious that Plato is directing our attention to "policy" within ourselves. After all, we cannot examine external policies until we have put our own internal policies in order.

This theme moves naturally on to the next, which is Plato's primary concern: the immortality of the soul. *The Republic* concludes with the tale of a hero named Er, risen from the dead after twelve days, who talks about what he has seen with his own eyes of the fate of the soul after death. This story reconfirms Plato's view that belief in immortality is essential to harmony and health of the soul. Here he comes very close to, though he does not actually enter, the realm of religion.

I have discussed Plato in such detail because I believe his idea of the ordering of the soul so that the rational part governs is a key point in establishing, firmly and widely, the age of the people's will and the tide of democracy. No authority, no matter how powerful, can go against the will of the people for very long.

Now the critical task we face is to divert the energy of liberation into the energy of building. We must begin by looking into ourselves, by examining, as Plato advocated, the "state within" even more rigorously than the "state without."

That process of introspection will, I believe, offer us important insights in defining the universal meaning of human rights. Articulating such a definition will both serve as a symbol of the movement for freedom and democracy and answer one of our most pressing needs for the twenty-first century.

The Art of Self-Mastery

The effects of mastering "the state within" can be awe-inspiring. For example, the great Renaissance man Leonardo da Vinci was in many respects the product of such self-mastery. Utterly free and independent, he was not only liberated from the strictures of religion and ethics but was also unconstrained by the bonds to nation, family, friends or acquaintances. He was a citizen of the world, untouchable and unsurpassed.

Leonardo was an illegitimate child and remained unmarried throughout his life. Little is known about his family, and his ties to the republic of Florence where he was born were weak. When he had completed his apprenticeship in Florence, he went right off to Milan, where he spent about seventeen years working under the patronage of its duke, Ludovico Sforza. Following Sforza's fall from power, Leonardo spent a short time working for the duke of Romagna, Cesare Borgia. He then moved to Florence, to Rome and back to Milan as his interests and projects led him.

Whatever his circumstance or course of action, Leonardo

showed little interest in the divisiveness of contemporary judgments on patriotism, personal allegiance or benefit. Instead, he strove to secure a style of life that would enable him to look upon all things with detachment. He paid no heed to the lures of fame and wealth, yet he was not a rebel against established authority. In his singular devotion to his own affairs, he was impervious to worldly convention.

Leonardo was not an unemotional person, nor did he lack virtue, but a transcendence of the mundane and the directed, single-minded pursuit of his calling define his life.

Leonardo was a multitalented genius of amazing versatility and breadth of interest. In addition to painting, he was a master sculptor, civil engineer and inventor of myriad devices ranging from flying machines to military weaponry. The same person who studied hydrodynamics and plant physiology, and who analyzed the flight of birds, also possessed an avid interest in human anatomy.

Whatever one can say about Leonardo, the scale of his mind was too grand to be measured by the norms of society. The freedom with which he rose above worldly concerns provides a glimpse of the truly liberated world citizen. Leonardo's life itself captures the unique freedom and vigor of the Italian Renaissance.

What allowed Leonardo to achieve such freedom was surely his mastery of the self. He wrote, "You can have neither a greater nor a lesser dominion than that over yourself."[5]

This was his first principle, upon which all others were

based. Self-mastery allowed him to respond flexibly to any reality. The conventional virtues of the day, such as loyalty and goodness, were of secondary importance to him. He had no qualms, for example, about accepting an invitation from Francis I to go to France, even though this was the king responsible for the downfall of Sforza, his previous patron. Was this a betrayal, a violation of integrity? I see in Leonardo's action, rather, a broad-minded acceptance and generosity of spirit.

Leonardo's ability to detach himself from convention reminds us of the Buddhist teaching of "transcending the world." "World" refers to the realm of differences, as between good and evil, love and hate, beauty and ugliness, advantage and disadvantage. "Transcending the world" is liberating oneself from attachments to all such distinctions.

The Lotus Sutra, Buddhism's highest teaching, speaks of the need to guide living beings and "cause them to renounce their attachments." Nichiren, whose teachings inspire the activities of the Soka Gakkai International, comments on this sutra and tells us: "The word *renounce* should be read *discern*." It's not enough simply to liberate ourselves from attachments; we must regard them clearly and carefully to see them for what they really are. Hence, "transcending the world" means establishing a strong inner self that will enable one to make proper use of any attachments.

The last words of the Buddha, Shakyamuni, were: "All phenomena are fleeting. Perfect your practice, never growing negligent." Nichiren also urges: "Strengthen your faith day by day and month after month. Should you slacken in your resolve even a bit, devils will take advantage."[6]

Another passage expresses life's deepest truth:

> This is similar to a tarnished mirror that will shine like a jewel when polished. A mind now clouded by the illusions of the innate darkness of life is like a tarnished mirror, but when polished, it is sure to become like a clear mirror, reflecting the essential nature of phenomena and the true aspect of reality.[7]

Detachment from the transient and illusory is one mark of character, which is another name for human wholeness or completeness. The principles to which I have been referring are not just abstractions but something that must be sought inwardly by people striving to grow in character.

Josei Toda emerged from a two-year imprisonment by the forces of Japanese militarism to initiate a new humanistic movement in Japan. He always focused on raising people of character, one person at a time, from among the populace. I have many fond memories of this compassionate man, whose love for youth knew no bounds and who encouraged us to be great actors on the stage of life. Indeed, the power of character is like the concentrated energy of an actor who has given himself or herself entirely over to the performance of the part. A person of outstanding character will always, even

under the most difficult circumstances, retain an air of com-
posure, ease and even humor. This is nothing other than the
achievement of self-mastery or self-control.

Goethe, who was an outstanding stage director in addition
to his other talents, was once asked what he looked for in an
actor, and he responded:

> Above all things, whether he had control over him-
> self. For an actor who possesses no self-possession,
> who cannot appear before a stranger in his most fa-
> vorable light, has, generally speaking, little talent.
> His whole profession requires continual self-denial.[8]

Goethe's idea of self-control corresponds to the concept
of moderation in Platonic philosophy. Self-control is not only
an essential quality for actors but is arguably the foremost
prerequisite for the development of character.

Character and "Human Revolution"

The question, then, remains: What can bring about a change
in character? In Buddhist practice, cultivating the awareness
of one's "life-condition" and making a diligent, constant
effort to elevate that condition constitute self-mastery, the
practice of "human revolution." A central teaching of Buddhist philosophy bears directly on the question of character
formation. As I mentioned earlier in this chapter, Buddhism

classifies the states or conditions of life that constitute human experience into what is termed the Ten Worlds or Realms. From the least to the most desirable they are: the world of Hell, a condition submerged in suffering; the world of Hunger, a state in which body and mind are engulfed in the raging flames of desire; the world of Animality, in which one fears the strong and abuses the weak; the world of Anger, characterized by the constant compulsion to surpass and dominate others; the world of Humanity, a tranquil state marked by the ability to make reasoned judgments; the world of Rapture, a state filled with joy; the world of Learning, a condition of aspiration to enlightenment; the world of Realization, where one perceives unaided the true nature of phenomena; the world of Bodhisattva, a state of compassion in which one seeks to save all people from suffering; and finally the world of Buddhahood, a state of human completeness and perfect freedom.

Within each of these ten states is likewise to be found the full spectrum of the Ten Worlds. In other words, the state of Hell contains within it every state from Hell to Buddhahood. In the Buddhist view, life is never static but is in constant flux, effecting a dynamic, moment-by-moment transformation among the states. The most critical point, then, is which of these ten states, as they exist in the vibrant flow of life, forms the basis for our individual lives? Buddhism offers a way of life centered on the highest states, those of Bodhisattva and Buddhahood, as an ideal of human existence.

Emotions — joy and sorrow, pleasure and anger — are of course the threads from which life's fabric is woven, and we continue to experience the full span of the Ten Worlds. These experiences, however, can be shaped and directed by the pure and indestructible states of Bodhisattva and Buddhahood.

The Soka Gakkai International is based on a philosophy of human revolution in which we hear echoes of Leonardo's spirit of self-mastery. Putting our beliefs into action, we support the United Nations and conduct many other activities for the cause of peace and culture, and through these efforts we contribute to society as a whole. At the same time, we stress the importance of inner reform in the individual. "You are your own master," Buddhist scripture says. "Could anyone else be your master? When you have gained control over yourself, you have found a master of rare value."[9]

A second passage reads: "Be lamps unto yourselves. Rely on yourselves. Hold fast to the Law as a lamp, do not rely on anything else."[10]

The Greater and Lesser Self

Both of the above passages urge us to live independently, true to ourselves and unswayed by others. The "self" referred to here, however, is not the Buddhist "lesser self," caught up in the snares of egoism. Rather, it is the "greater self," fused with the life of the universe through which cause and effect intertwine over the infinite reaches of space and time.

The greater, cosmic self is related to the unifying and integrating "self" that Jung perceived in the depths of the ego. It is also similar to Ralph Waldo Emerson's "universal beauty, to which every part and particle is equally related; the eternal One."[11]

I am firmly convinced that a large-scale awakening to the greater self will lead to a world of creative coexistence in the coming century. Recall the lines of Walt Whitman, in which he sings the praises of the human spirit:

> But that I,
> turning to thee O soul,
> thou actual Me,
> And lo, thou gently masterest the orbs,
> Thou matest Time,
> smilest content at Death,
> And fillest,
> swellest full the vastness of space.[12]

The greater self of Mahayana Buddhism is another way of expressing the openness and expansiveness of character that embrace the sufferings of all people as one's own. This self always seeks ways of alleviating the pain and augmenting the happiness of others, here, amid the realities of everyday life. Only the solidarity brought about by such natural human nobility will break down the isolation of the modern self and lead to the dawning of new hope for civilization. Furthermore, the dynamic, vital awakening of the greater self will enable each of us, as individuals, to experience both life and death with equal delight. Thus, as Nichiren stated: "We adorn the treasure tower of our being with the four aspects of birth, aging, sickness and death."[13]

If we are in sufficient command of ourselves, we will not feel compelled to impose our own values upon others nor to trample upon the customs and values they hold dear. Self-control also prevents us from trying to rationalize everything in economic terms regardless of the conditions, perceptions and ramifications of other countries, saving us from being relegated to the ignoble company of economic animals.

Respect for All Humanity

In the Lotus Sutra, there is a bodhisattva named Never Disparaging. This bodhisattva believed that since all humans possess the Buddha nature, none could be despised; that all life, all humanity, had to be accorded the highest respect. Even when proud and boastful people denounced the bodhisattva, struck him with their staffs and pelted him with stones, he still refused to disdain them, believing that to belittle them would be to belittle the Buddha. He continued to preach this doctrine to the end, honoring respect for humanity in his every word and deed.

Bodhisattva Never Disparaging's unshakable belief that

humanity should never be despised exemplifies the kind of self-control we must learn to nurture in ourselves. In the Lotus Sutra, the story of Bodhisattva Never Disparaging is a parable of the ultimate in Buddhist discipline. It also is akin to Plato's contention that we must learn to place our souls under the control of our "rational part" and illustrates the importance of self-control as a universal virtue of all humankind and the primary requirement for a world without war.

3
chapter

THE PATH OF
DIALOGUE AND TOLERANCE

chapter

3 THE PATH OF DIALOGUE AND TOLERANCE

THE REAL SEEDS OF PEACE lie not in lofty ideas but in human understanding and the empathy of ordinary people.

While radicalism is fated by its nature to resort to violence and terror, the most potent weapon in the arsenal of the gradualist — the radical's opposite — is dialogue. We see in Socrates the steadfast commitment to dialogue, to verbal combat from which there is no retreat, and an intensity that is, in some literal sense, death-defying. Such dialogue can only be sustained by resources of spiritual energy and strength far greater and deeper than will be found among those who so quickly turn to violence.

Only within the open space created by dialogue, whether conducted with our neighbors, with history, with nature or the cosmos, can human wholeness be sustained. The closed silence of the disengaged can only become the site of spiritual suicide. We are not born human in any but a biological sense; we can only learn to know ourselves and others and thus be trained in the ways of being human. We do this by immersion in the ocean of language and dialogue fed by the springs of cultural tradition.

I am reminded again of the beautiful and moving passage in *Phaedo* in which Plato describes Socrates teaching his youthful disciples how hatred of language and ideas leads to antipathy toward humanity. Mistrust of language is but the inverse of an excessive belief in the power of language. The two are different aspects of the same thing, which is a frailty of spirit in which one cannot cope with the stresses of human proximity brought about by dialogue. This sort of spiritual weakness causes a person to vacillate between undue trustfulness and suspicion of other people, thus becoming easy prey for the forces of disintegration.

Our efforts for the sake of dialogue, in order to be worthy of the term *dialogue*, must be carried through to the end. To refuse peaceful exchange and choose force is to compromise and give in to human weakness; it is to admit the defeat of the human spirit. Socrates encourages his youthful disciples to train and strengthen themselves spiritually, to maintain hope and self-control, to advance courageously, choosing virtue over material wealth, truth over fame.

While we cannot regard modern mass society in terms of the values of ancient Greece, we must not overemphasize the differences between them. In his classic study, *Public Opinion*, one of the greatest journalists of the twentieth century, Walter Lippmann, for one, repeatedly calls for Socratic dialogue and Socratic individuals as the keys to the more wholesome formation of public opinion. Education based on open dialogue is far more than the mere transfer of information and knowledge; it enables us to rise above the confines of our parochial perspectives and passions. Institutes of higher learning are charged with the task of encouraging Socratic world citizens and spearheading the search for new principles for the peaceful integration of our world.

Buddhism and the Power of Dialogue

Shakyamuni Buddha, who is often mentioned with Socrates as one of the world's great teachers, spent the last moments of his life exhorting his grieving disciples to engage him in dialogue. To the very end, he continued to urge them to question him on any subject, as one friend to another.

Since its inception, the philosophy of Buddhism has been associated with peace and pacifism. That emphasis derives principally from the consistent rejection of violence combined with stress on dialogue and discussion as the best means to resolve conflict. Descriptions of Shakyamuni's life provide a good illustration. His life was completely untrammeled by dogma, and his interactions with his fellows stressed the importance of dialogue. The sutra recounting the travels that culminated his Buddhist practice begins with an episode in which the aged Shakyamuni uses the power of language to avert an invasion.

According to the sutra, Shakyamuni, then eighty years

old, did not directly admonish the minister of Magadha, a large country bent on conquering the neighboring state of Vaji. Instead, he spoke persuasively about the principles by which nations prosper and decline. His discourse dissuaded the minister from carrying out the planned attack. The final chapter of the same sutra concludes with a moving description of Shakyamuni on his deathbed. As he lay dying, he repeatedly urges his disciples to raise any uncertainties that they might have about the Buddhist law (dharma) or its practice so that they would not find themselves regretting unasked questions after his death. Up until his last moment, Shakyamuni actively sought out dialogue, and the drama of his final voyage from beginning to end is illuminated by the light of language, skillfully wielded by one who was truly a "master of words."[1]

Attachment to Differences

Why could Shakyamuni employ language with such freedom and to such effect? What made him such a peerless master of dialogue? I believe his fluency was due to the expansiveness of his enlightened state, utterly free of dogma, prejudice and attachment. The following quote is illustrative: "I perceived a single, invisible arrow piercing the hearts of the people."[2] The "arrow" symbolizes a prejudicial mindset, an unreasoning emphasis on individual differences. India at that time was going through transition and upheaval, and the horrors of

conflict and war were an ever-present reality. To Shakyamuni's penetrating gaze, it was clear that the underlying
cause of the conflict was attachment to distinctions, to ethnic, national and other differences.

In the early years of the twentieth century, philosopher
Josiah Royce declared that: "Reform, in such matters, must
come, if at all, from within.... The public as a whole is whatever the processes that occur, for good or evil, in individual
minds, may determine."[3]

As Royce points out, the "invisible arrow" of evil is not to
be found in the existence of races and classes external to
ourselves but is embedded in our hearts. The conquest of
our own prejudicial thinking, our own attachment to difference, is the necessary precondition for open dialogue. Such
discussion, in turn, is essential for the establishment of peace
and universal respect for human rights. Shakyamuni's complete absence of prejudice enabled him to expound the law
with such freedom, adapting his style of teaching to the character and capacity of the person to whom he was speaking.

Whether mediating a communal dispute over water
rights, converting a violent criminal or admonishing someone who objected to the practice of begging, Shakyamuni
attempted first to make others aware of the "arrow" of their
inner evil. The power of his extraordinary character brought
these words to the lips of one contemporaneous sovereign:
"Those whom we, with weapons, cannot force to surrender,
you subdue unarmed."[4]

The power of the word is the primary weapon of the champion of the spirit. Long described as the single characteristic most clearly differentiating humans from other animals, language has often been the decisive factor in victory. History is filled with bloody battles among peoples enslaved by the powers of brutality, authority and money. But, even in the desolate and barren landscape of conflict and killing, a few instances in which the power of the word has led to victory stand out. The American Revolution, without which American democracy would have been impossible, is one of the most outstanding examples. In the case of the American Revolution, the abilities of self-control, balance and self-regulation, which I believe are indispensable for manifesting the spirit as a force for good, resulted in tendencies different from those observable in the French and Russian revolutions.

The Word and Revolution

On the eve and in the early stages of all the major modern revolutions — the American, French and the Russian — the word was used to spread the cause. In *Ten Days That Shook the World*, his outstanding on-the-scene reportage of the Russian Revolution, the American journalist John Reed vividly describes this:

All Russia was learning to read, and *reading* — politics, economics, history — because the people

wanted to *know*.... In every city, in most towns, along
the front, each political faction had its newspaper
—sometimes several. Hundreds of thousands of
pamphlets were distributed by thousands of organizations, and poured into the armies, the villages,
the factories, the streets. The thirst for education, so
long thwarted, burst with the Revolution into a
frenzy of expression. From Smolny Institute alone,
the first six months, went out every day, tons, car-
loads, train-loads of literature, saturating the land.
Russia absorbed reading matter like hot sand drinks
water, insatiable. And it was not fables, falsified
history, diluted religion, and the cheap fiction that
corrupts—but social and economic theories, philosophy, the works of Tolstoy, Gogol, Gorky....[5]

This quotation brilliantly describes a vast upsurge of
energy among a people newly armed with the word. Something similar occurred in the early stages of the French Revolution. Unfortunately, however, in both instances, the
violent train of later events mercilessly suppressed that
energy. Tyranny and terror ousted and replaced freedom of
speech. Silence was enforced on the people, and the spirit
was defeated.

In America, on the other hand, as the classic analysis by the
French historian Alexis de Tocqueville makes clear, the town
meetings that characterized the early New England were a

seedbed for the cultivation of grass-roots democracy. The energy of the township at the time of the American Revolution was directed both toward the present, in the form of striving for independence, and toward the future, in the form of the search for an independent political order. Energy for the sake of liberation was at the same time constructive: During the struggle to break from England, all thirteen of the original colonies were writing their own constitutions. The state of Virginia was at the same time drawing up the Virginia Bill of Rights, which remains a model of its kind.

Words and the "Abstract Spirit"

Words can be detached from the service of communication, dialogue, and their force subverted into justifying an inhuman cause. This is the fallacy of placing ideology above the personal, human reality — sacrificing lives to the "abstract spirit." Again, Gabriel Marcel elaborates:

> From the moment that one (be it the State or a party, a faction or religious sect) claims to agree with me that I am committing an act of war on other beings whom I must be ready to annihilate, it is utterly necessary that I lose awareness of the individual existence of the being I may bring into submission. To transform him into a whipping boy, it is absolutely necessary to convert him into an

abstraction, such as the communist, the fascist, or the non-fascist, etc.[6]

This certainly seems reasonable. Whether at war or not, people are not so easily drawn into committing violence against others if they sense the others' concrete, personal existence. This is especially true among people who know well and live near one another.

Prejudice and Stereotyping

To motivate people to make war, that abstraction, the Enemy, needs to be cloaked in a recognizable costume: the stereotype. Lippmann incisively analyzed the problem of how easily belief can lead, through stereotypes, to a distorted perception of the world around us. Lippmann made his living as a journalist, an occupation Marcel disparaged for its "almost invariably...corrupting effect." Lippmann's *Public Opinion* is a work of conscience, the self-admonishing effort of a journalist to expose the deepest sources of the malaise that afflicted civilization in the twentieth century.

Observing that "Whatever we recognize as familiar we tend, if we are not very careful, to visualize with the aid of images already in our mind," Lippmann goes on to say:

Except where we deliberately keep prejudice in suspense, we do not study a man and judge him to be

bad. We see a bad man. We see a dewy morn, a blush-
ing maiden, a sainted priest, a humorless English-
man, a dangerous Red, a carefree bohemian, a lazy
Hindu, a wily Oriental, a dreaming Slav, a volatile
Irishman, a greedy Jew, a 100 percent American.[7]

For Lippmann, public opinion is corrupted from the outset by these stereotypes. Though public opinion may, like
nationalism, be considered a reflection of popular will, there
are innumerable instances where the people have been mes-
merized by stereotype-based sloganeering and sent into violent rampages unthinkable under normal circumstances.
Lippmann asserts that what characterizes public opinion in
mass society is that stereotypes make the average man "dog-
matic, because his belief is a complete myth."

Ideologies such as communism have produced in prodi-
gious quantity a peculiar kind of character: ideologues who
are superficial, intolerant and self-righteous. It is impossible
to engage in true dialogue with those who are closed-minded
and intolerant. As long as they remain shut up within their
myths, no matter how much they may talk — indeed, the
more long-winded and bombastic they are — they are inca-
pable of carrying on a dialogue, only a monologue.

The Revolt of the Masses

When we speak of the theory of mass society in the twentieth century, we cannot forget one other person who has earned an honored place as a pioneer thinker: José Ortega y Gasset. Some people believe his principal work, *The Revolt of the Masses*, has the same significance for the twentieth century that Jean-Jacques Rousseau's *The Social Contract* had for the eighteenth and Karl Marx's *Das Kapital* had for the nineteenth. From the heights of a noble spirit, Ortega focuses his extraordinary critical powers on an analysis of that uniquely twentieth-century phenomenon — the ascendancy of the masses. This work is filled with valuable insights for us today, well over half a century after its writing. Ortega, too, placed great importance on dialogue as a pivotal factor in the creation of culture.

Without fixed rules to guide us, however, we cannot engage in dialogue; in fact, it is precisely those shared rules that constitute the underlying principle of culture. According to Ortega:

> When all these things are lacking there is no culture; there is in the strictest sense of the word, barbarism. And let us not deceive ourselves, this is what is beginning to appear in Europe under the progressive rebellion of the masses.[8]

The word *masses*, as used here, does not refer to a specific social stratum. Ortega's "mass-man" is a new breed of human being, someone he calls a "new Adam" and a "self-satisfied" child. The structure of his soul is built on two fundamental characteristics: a "hermetism" that derives from his intoxication with self-satisfaction and a shallow sense of victory and an "indocility" that cause him to go his own way without regard to rules or norms.

Hermetism and Indocility

Hermetism and indocility are the two aspects that make up this self-satisfied child's peculiar form of infantilism, which, like a two-edged sword, severs the ties of dialogue that otherwise exist among mature people. Ortega's words are a warning that clearly anticipates the isolation and withdrawal from human relations that have come to afflict contemporary mass society.

The following passage from *The Revolt of the Masses* analyzes the mentality of the mass-man.

> This contentment with himself leads him to shut himself off from any external court of appeal; not to listen, not to submit his opinions to judgment, not to consider others' existence. His intimate feeling of power urges him always to exercise predominance.

He will act then as if he and his like were the only beings existing in the world.... [9]

This is truly a portrait of a person enslaved by a closed
mind, a state that is in turn the source of the civilizational
afflictions discussed here: an absence of critical thinking leading to fanaticism and intolerance.

Gabriel Marcel, Walter Lippmann and José Ortega y Gasset were contemporaries. Their writings illustrate the same
profound concern: that closed-mindedness robs people of
the ability to engage in dialogue and discourse with others
—a capacity that can be considered proof of our humanity
—and that this was the cause of the serious ills they
observed around them.

This exclusivist impulse has afflicted human society since
the dawn of history, a predisposition criticized by French
philosopher Henri Bergson as the tendency toward a "closed
society" and more recently by American essayist Norman
Cousins as a "tribal consciousness." In a closed society, all
may go well within the group itself, but as contact is made
with other cultures or societies, its members shut themselves
off, refusing to participate in the very debate and dialogue
that are proof of their humanity. Ultimately, they resort to
violence. When two cultures meet and either one or both
cannot tolerate the other's culture or way of life, the resultant friction need only rise to a certain degree before the two
clash head-on.

Overcoming negative attachments to difference—discrimination—and bringing about a true flowering of human diversity are the keys to generating a lasting culture of peace. And dialogue is the means to achieve this active tolerance.

Montaigne and Tolerance

One eminent thinker best suited to the discussion of tolerance is Montaigne. The great thinker was above all a firm believer in the importance of dialogue, repeatedly stating that discussion provided the best means for people to hammer out their differences and to pursue personal growth and discipline.

Montaigne lived in sixteenth-century France, where religious strife spawned numerous tragedies, including the St. Bartholomew Massacre of 1572 during the wars of the Huguenots. In his *Essays*, he notes how zeal is plentiful when it comes to furthering our inclinations toward hatred, cruelty, ambition, avarice, criticism or rebellion, but when we seek to be good, benign or temperate, it is apt to be in short supply. And he deplores the fact that though religion was intended to root out vice, instead it often provokes, even encourages or aggravates evil.

Living as he did in the midst of religious turmoil, and often witnessing people killing one another for the sake of personal gain and fanatical beliefs, Montaigne urged tolerance as the key to stopping the fighting. After his death, his doctrine was embodied in the Edict of Nantes (1598), which recognized the right of heretics to freely practice their religious beliefs. Further, his report that Christians establishing colonies overseas were far more brutal than the idolatrous native populations they encountered, and that they committed deeds that were far less moral, helped to promote what would now be termed *religious relativism*. It is often pointed out that Montaigne's observations shocked contemporary Christians of good faith and moved many toward personal introspection. The Austrian writer Stefan Zweig left us a resounding endorsement of Montaigne's doctrine and thought when he said that Montaigne was the friend of all free people.

In any event, dialogue was of utmost importance to Montaigne in the context of those tumultuous times. He believed that "the most fruitful and natural exercise for our minds is, in my opinion, conversation. I find the practice of it pleasanter than anything else in life." Defining an open mind as an absolute condition for conversation, he observed that "no proposition astounds me, no belief offends me, however much opposed it may be to my own. There is no fantasy so frivolous or extravagant that it does not seem to me a natural product of the human mind." He also asserted: "Contradictions of opinion, therefore, neither offend nor estrange me; they only arouse and exercise my mind. We run away from correction; we ought to court it and expose ourselves to it, especially when it comes in the shape of discussion, not of a school lesson."[10]

Montaigne took to heart Cicero's assertion that no debate was possible without rebuttal, and he went on to define the purpose of dialogue as the search for truth: "I welcome and embrace the truth in whosoever hands I find it. I cheerfully surrender to it, and offer it my vanquished arms as soon as I see it approaching in the distance."[11] Through sentiments such as these, Montaigne reveals himself as a true spiritual king and a shining example of towering integrity engaged in open discussion.

To these observations, I would add that a lively spirit of criticism is also indispensable at the foundation of dialogue. The confrontation between Protestantism and Catholicism ripped French society apart in Montaigne's era. There were repeated massacres on both sides, but in the midst of that madness Montaigne managed to live his life on his own terms. His unyielding spirit is described in Zweig's critical biography:

> Few men on earth have fought with more sincerity and vehemence for this innermost self, their essence to be kept away from the murky and poisonous froth of the times, and few men have succeeded in saving their innermost self from the times.[12]

Montaigne himself said it was useless to engage in dialogue with those whose views were not supported by rational, critical ability. He saw no purpose in discussion with those undisciplined or wavering in what they believed. He also stated that this ability to think critically included the capacity for rigorous self-examination.

The Buddhist Approach to Dialogue

True dialogue is only possible when both parties are committed to self-mastery. But there is another essential element without which dialogue becomes manipulative rhetoric: respectful compassion for the other—no matter how culturally different they are from oneself or seemingly opposed to one's own interest. The Buddhist approach can, I believe, loosen the shackles of abstract concepts and language that can be so destructive. Thus freed, we can use language to the greatest effect and can engage in the kind of dialogue that creates the greatest and most lasting value. Dialogue must be pivotal in our endeavors, reaching out to all people everywhere as we seek to forge a new global civilization.

Nichiren's faith in the power of language was absolute. If more people were to pursue dialogue in an equally unrelenting manner, the inevitable conflicts of human life would surely find easier resolution. Prejudice would yield to empathy, and war would give way to peace. Genuine dialogue results in the transformation of opposing viewpoints, changing them from wedges that drive people apart into bridges that link them together.

The human qualities necessary to put this principle into

practice go beyond mere diplomacy; the task requires an elevated state of life. What the Lotus Sutra describes as a Bodhisattva of the Earth is a person committed to the work of restoring a sense of cosmology to contemporary society. In concrete terms, this means being a master of the art of dialogue and a standard-bearer of soft power. The Lotus Sutra summarizes the characteristics these bodhisattvas must have as follows:

> Firm in the power of will and concentration,
> with constant diligence seeking wisdom,
> they expound various wonderful doctrines
> and their minds are without fear.
> They are clever at difficult questions and answers,
> their minds know no fear.
> They have firmly cultivated a persevering mind,
> upright in dignity and virtue.[13]

Fear builds barriers of aversion and discrimination in the forms of national boundaries or of exclusion and discrimination on the bases of race, religion, gender, social class, financial status or merely personal preference. As Lippmann pointed out, to shore up and gloss over their prejudices, people with closed minds often stereotype others. This attitude reflects a mental indolence that stops us from cultivating mutual understanding and trust or developing the perseverance and determination required to engage in dialogue. As history teaches, it is only a short step from mental laziness to violence. In praising the Bodhisattvas of the Earth for their total lack of fear, therefore, the sutra commends their efforts to transcend all discriminatory barriers and their readiness to engage in dialogue without hesitation. The tone of this dialogue is modulated to suit the moods and needs of the occasion. Sometimes, their words can be like a healing breeze, sometimes like a rousing beat, sometimes like an awakening peal, and sometimes like a sword that slashes through delusion. Their efforts at dialogue are supported by their firm conviction in the fundamental equality of all people — that all people possess the potential for enlightenment.

A profound faith in humanity inspires the Bodhisattvas of the Earth to constantly dedicate themselves to dialogue in the effort to find common ground and harmonize different perspectives.

The following three traits summarize the character and mentality of the Bodhisattvas of the Earth:

- To be rigorously strict toward oneself, like a sharp autumn frost.
- To be warm and embracing toward others, like a soft spring breeze.
- To be uncompromising when confronting evil, like a lion monarch.

Only a person embodying these traits can be a master of

dialogue. The bodhisattva vows to save others and bases all action upon this vow, which is a spontaneous expression of altruism. Nor is the vow a mere expression of determination or desire but a defining commitment to whose realization the bodhisattva devotes his or her entire being. The bodhisattva refuses to be dissuaded or discouraged by the difficulties posed by this challenge. The Lotus Sutra speaks of the pure white lotus rising from the waters of a muddy pond. This analogy illustrates the attainment of a pure and empowered state of life in the midst of the sometimes-degrading realities of human society. In this way, the bodhisattva never tries to escape from reality, never leaves suffering people unsaved and instead plunges into life's turbulent waters in the effort to help each person drowning in suffering onto the great vessel of happiness.

The Nature of Dialogue

Dialogue is not limited to formal debate or placid exchange that wafts by like a spring breeze. There are times when, to break the grip of arrogance, speech must be like the breath of fire. Thus, although we typically associate Shakyamuni Buddha only with mildness, he spoke out with great ferocity when it was warranted.

Similarly, Nichiren, who demonstrated a familial affection and tender concern for the common people, was uncompromising in his confrontations with corrupt and degenerate authority. Always unarmed in the chronically violent Japan of his time, he relied exclusively and unflinchingly on the power of persuasion and nonviolence. He was promised power if he renounced his faith and threatened with the beheading of his parents if he adhered to his beliefs. Nevertheless, he maintained the courage of his convictions. The following passage, written upon his exile to a distant island from which none was expected to return, typifies his leonine tone: "Whatever obstacles I might encounter, so long as persons of wisdom do not prove my teachings to be false, I will never yield!" [14]

Nichiren took a course of action that could be expected only of someone dedicated to the salvation of the whole human race. He worked to clarify philosophical right from wrong and to remove the evils that torment people. His weapon of choice in that task was discussion, the sole weapon for the enlightened.

When dialogue is pursued in the spirit or with the intention of influencing others, it is impossible to proceed without discussing the issues of right and wrong, good and evil. This is because, as Montaigne says, the ultimate purpose of dialogue is to search for the truth, and the mutual critique developed by the participants thereby represents the sublime manifestation of the human spirit.

When I was young, Josei Toda told us that "Young people are the core of Japan, because they are the ones with keen critical abilities." His fervent wish was to erase misery from the face of the earth, and he exhorted the young to fight the many evils afflicting people by thoroughly training themselves to think critically.

Tolerance does not mean unprincipled compromise. No matter how extensive the dialogue, nothing creative and constructive will be accomplished if we focus our attention solely on discovering points of compromise without attempting to discriminate good from evil and lose the ability to think critically. On the contrary, such an approach is a betrayal of the quintessentially human desire to seek the truth.

The Nature of the Greater Self

Of course, endless assertions of one's own ideas can degenerate into self-righteousness and prejudice, as history so tragically and eloquently attests. How can we overcome this historical dilemma?

As I mentioned earlier, I believe the answer lies in developing the greater self as taught in Mahayana Buddhism. Buddhist scriptures tell us that the self is its own master. They enjoin us not to be confused by others but instead to live our lives with integrity, remaining true to ourselves. Again, however, this "self" does not refer to the lesser self or ego but to the greater self that is fused with cosmic life in a web of causal relationships beyond all temporal and spatial limits. This greater self is another name for the openness that identifies

with the suffering of all sentient beings. In the course of dealing with people in society, one who develops the greater self
can "take away suffering and give happiness."This way of life
is precisely what Nichiren risked his life to exemplify and is
the model so fervently pursued by Josei Toda.

The greater self is the key, I believe, to realizing the tolerance that makes genuine dialogue possible. Tolerance can
help us create a new epoch of coexistence, shining the light
of hope into the dark shroud of pessimism.

Dialogue in Politics

If we take a hard look at the world today, we can discern a
new current already at work beneath the violent waves of
change. As I see it, we are on the threshold of a new age of
dialogue. For years I have been calling for genuine dialogue
among the top leaders of major powers. They ought to meet
for the frank and constructive exchange of views, rise above
their differences of ideology and social system, and free
themselves from preconceptions. Only then can the foundations for peace in the twenty-first century be laid.

More than thirty years after Daniel Bell first coined the
phrase "the end of ideology," we are finally witnessing the
burgeoning of a new perspective that, going beyond differences of system and ideology, considers the earth as a single,
interconnected whole. It is said that President Franklin D.
Roosevelt, attending the Yalta Conference, was determined

to follow Emerson's admonition: "The only way to make a friend is to be one." I, for one, believe that when the political world loses sight of the Emersonian kind of idealism it is destined to degenerate into the world of beasts that Plato envisaged.

The Soka Gakkai International remains committed to the role of dialogue in the advancement of peace, education and culture. At present, we are engaged in forging bonds of solidarity with citizens in 163 countries and regions around the world.

To put this into actual practice, we have sought to promote dialogue among civilizations, meeting with individuals from every continent on earth. I have held discussions with intellectual leaders from various religious backgrounds — Christianity, Islam, Hinduism, Judaism, etc. — and these conversations have often been published. Based on years of such experience, I am keenly aware of the possibilities of open dialogue and the importance of its implications in society.

The Mystic Law (*myoho*), which forms the basis of the SGI's belief, is written with the Chinese character *myo*, which has three meanings: "to open," "to be endowed" and "to revive." As the first meaning suggests, the SGI is engaged in a Buddhist movement to open the closed hearts and minds at the root of civilization's decline.

The SGI aims not simply to treat the superficial symptoms

of the malaise but to take on the challenging task of rooting out its very causes. Symptomatic treatment is of course indispensable for dealing with emergencies such as the frequent eruptions of ethnic strife. But if we do not also turn our attention to the underlying causes, our actions will be no more than frantic attempts to cope with immediate crises, like trying to stamp out one fire as another is started.

Josei Toda advocated the idea of the global family at a time when the tensions of the Cold War were intensifying, and few paid attention to his ideas. At best, they were dismissed as unrealistic reveries. But today, this idea has finally entered the public consciousness as "transnationalism," which has become a key concept in explaining and predicting the future direction of global affairs. Observing this trend, we can only appreciate even more the remarkable foresight of Mr. Toda.

Although we have not yet taken even the first step toward creating a system that can accommodate the new era our world has entered, there is general agreement that the United Nations should play a central role in building a new global order of peace. It seems that, in the words of former Secretary-General Boutros Boutros-Ghali, "an opportunity has been regained to achieve the objectives of the Charter— a United Nations capable of maintaining international peace and security, of securing justice and human rights and of promoting, in the words of the Charter, 'social progress and better standards of life in larger freedom.'"[15]

SGI Efforts To Promote Tolerance

SGI organizations around the world carry out activities to create peace in their respective areas in accordance with a principle of the SGI Charter: "The SGI shall, based on the Buddhist spirit of tolerance, respect other religions, engage in dialogue and work together with them towards the resolution of fundamental issues concerning humanity." The SGI has also promoted interfaith dialogue by sponsoring symposiums and other forums with institutions such as the European Academy of Sciences and Arts.

In recent years our representatives have attended the Parliament of the World's Religions in Cape Town, South Africa, in 1999 and the Millennium World Peace Summit of Religious and Spiritual Leaders in 2000 at the U.N. Headquarters in New York.

The SGI-affiliated Boston Research Center for the 21st Century has published *Subverting Hatred: The Challenge of Nonviolence in Religious Traditions*, a collection of essays by scholars representing various religions that discusses the philosophies of nonviolence found in eight of the world's religious traditions and ways to overcome conflict.

In addition, the Institute of Oriental Philosophy has been making multidimensional efforts toward dialogue among religions. The Toda Institute for Global Peace and Policy Research recently held an international conference on the theme "Dialogue of Civilizations: A New Peace Agenda for a

New Millennium," gathering together experts to discuss major civilizations and their underlying religious dimensions. As founder of the institute, I have been engaged in discussions with its director, Professor Majid Tehranian of the University of Hawaii, toward promoting dialogue between two of the world's major religious cultures, Islam and Buddhism. Professor Tehranian has written that the world today is "endowed with expanding channels of communication yet sorely in need of dialogue." Undeniably, in our information-saturated society, we are being inundated by ready-made stereotypes obscuring the truth of people and situations. This is why person-to-person dialogue — always the basis of dialogue among civilizations — is more than ever in demand.

I am convinced that we can solve any problem as long as we keep our minds open and stand firm in our belief in our common humanity.

Tolerance is more than just a mental attitude; it must grow out of a sense of larger order and coexistence, a cosmic sensibility that issues up from the deepest wellsprings of life. As explained by the Buddhist doctrine of "dependent origination," no phenomenon in either the human or natural domains arises independently of all others. The cosmos is created through the interrelation and interdependence of all things. Tolerance rooted in a world view of dynamic interdependence can, I believe, be instrumental in enabling us to transcend the threat of a clash of civilizations and to realize a philosophy of coexistence that will permit us to build a world of human harmony.

4
chapter

THE PATH

OF COMMUNITY

4 THE PATH
OF COMMUNITY

WHAT IMPACT do individuals devoted to self-mastery and committed to dialogue have on the values underlying current systems of economics, politics, education, culture and religion in their communities?

Economics and Humanitarian Competition

A ruthless struggle for economic domination takes place beyond the regulatory reach of national governments and under the slogan of "free market" principles. The problem is not capitalism per se but indifference to both global justice and ethical standards.

In *The Geography of Human Life,* published at the beginning of the twentieth century, Tsunesaburo Makiguchi described shifts in modes of national competition—from military to political to economic. Moving from the descriptive to the predictive, he set out a vision of what he termed "humanitarian competition," which represents a profound qualitative transformation of competition itself, toward a model that recognizes our interrelatedness and emphasizes the cooperative aspects of living. He envisaged a time in which people and countries would compete—in the original sense of the words *striving together*—to make the greatest contribution to human happiness and well-being.[1]

From this context, he maintained that the ultimate goal of a state lies in the accomplishment of humanitarianism, and he asserted that nations should always adhere to noncoercive, intangible (i.e., nonmilitary, noneconomic) means to expand their sphere of influence. In this sense, Makiguchi could be said to have identified with foresight and wisdom what we now know as soft power, the ability to win naturally the hearts and minds of people.

I am drawn to Makiguchi's vision in that he does more than predict a shift in the modes and locus of competition; he foresees and requires a transformation in the very nature of competition, from that whose essence is confrontation to that whose baseline is cooperation.

The global gap between rich and poor was once discussed in terms of the rich North versus the poor South. Today, however, against a backdrop of increasingly fierce global economic competition, we find strains between strong and weak, winners and losers, within both North and South, as well as within individual countries around the globe. The stark realities of an "eat or be eaten" world draw into question the very meaning and intent of a civilization whose acknowledged commitment has always been to progress. Certainly, in this regard, Makiguchi's admonition that it is time to vie with one another not for power or money but for achievement of humanitarian goals offers the kind of far-sighted vision around which we may successfully order humankind's affairs in this new millennium.

At the heart of humanitarian competition is the extension of the spiritual influence — of cultural achievement and moral persuasion — that a country or people exerts on the world. In today's terms this might be described as expansion of our soft-power competitiveness. Makiguchi writes:

> Military and political power — sometimes under the cloak of economic strength — that pursues territo-rial expansion, seeking to place as many people as possible under its influence, should be supplanted by those intangible forces that naturally inspire peo-ple's respect.... Rather than responding to the force of threat, people will offer their support willingly and without reserve.[2]

He continues:

> There is no simple formula for this humanitarian-ism. Rather, all activities, whether in the realm of politics or of economics, should be conducted in conformity with the principles of humanitarianism.

> What is important is to eschew egotistical actions, striving to protect and improve not only your own life but others' as well. One should do things for the sake of others, for by benefiting others, we benefit ourselves. This means, in other words, to engage consciously in collective life.[3]

He thus suggests that humanitarian competition will influence other forms of competition, which will in turn bring about a shift in people's consciousness from competition to coexistence and cooperation.

Reexamining the Meaning of Competition

The Group of Lisbon, an international council that presents policy recommendations, includes the noteworthy observation in its publication *Limits to Competition* that although competition originally meant "seeking together," it has come to denote defeating or triumphing over others. As this example indicates, we hear more and more voices calling for a reexamination of the meaning of competition.[4]

The Buddhist concept of interdependence supports this notion of a humanistic economy. A Buddhist analogy illustrates the idea: Long ago, in India, there was a tradition of binding twenty or thirty long, slender reeds together into a bundle. Shariputra, a disciple of the Buddha, famous for his unparalleled wisdom, first employed the analogy of the two bundles of reeds.

"Let us suppose that there are two bundles of reeds," Shariputra said. "As long as the two are leaning against each other, they stand up. In the same way, because there is a 'this,' there can be a 'that,' and because there is a 'that,' there can be a 'this.'" But if we take away one of the bundles of reeds, the other will fall over.

The Buddhist canon gives us another beautiful image of the cosmic view of history, showing how all the phenomena of the universe interrelate, producing a perfect, subtle harmony: "Suspended above the palace of Indra, the Buddhist god who symbolizes the natural forces that protect and nurture life, is an enormous net. A brilliant jewel is attached to each knot in the net. Each jewel contains and reflects the image of all the other jewels in the net, which sparkles in the magnificence of its totality."

This poignant image illustrates the concept of "dependent origination." Dependent origination is the fundamental Buddhist doctrine that teaches the coexistence of all things in the universe, including human beings and nature, in interdependent relationships. It expounds the symbiosis of the *micro*cosmos and the *macro*cosmos that unite as one organism.

The idea goes far beyond the mechanistic view of the world removed from humanity, which formed the background for modern science. I emphasize here that Buddhism sees the relationships of all things in the universe not as a still, static image but as the dynamic pulsing of creative life.

People — communities, nations — cannot exist in isolation; they depend upon one another for help. The building of a world community, a global civilization of justice, compassion and hope must begin by turning away from the "eat or be eaten" ethos of competition and cultivating in its place a shared ethos of cooperation and interdependence. This, in fact, is closer to the original sense of the word *competition*.

The Spirit of Fairness

How does this global awareness manifest in the way an individual conducts business? I have long cherished the saying, "Control your business; don't let it control it you." By its very nature, business is geared to economic efficiency and the pursuit of profit. A businessman who works strictly for the good of his enterprise alone will think only in terms of the bottom line. That narrow focus has given rise on occasion to competition so excessive as to blow up in military conflict. If business activities are to contribute to efforts toward peace, the logic of capital must be tempered by the logic of humanity.

How can this be achieved? In Japanese there is a word *kosei*, which may be translated as "the spirit of fairness." It also means equality and impartiality, as well as justice. A person with the spirit of fairness recognizes the inherent contradiction in economic activity that makes the rich richer and the poor poorer, both on the individual and national levels. Such a person clearly recognizes the insidious threat of economic growth that thrives at the expense of the global environment and the delicate balance of the ecosystem. The "export" of pollution to countries with less strict regulations, for example, is anathema to people who place justice and equality first.

The spirit of fairness or justice is not an *a priori* condition. Through tough challenges, the spirit of fairness is transformed from the ethos of a people into a universal principle endowed with the strength of steel, the warmth of the sun and the vastness of the sky. A true sense of fairness must be derived from a universal spirit manifested on this higher plane. In the world of business, such a universal spirit would not be preoccupied with the good of one's own venture or nation. It would always consider the greater, holistic interest of the entire planet and of all humankind and thereby inspire one to make impartial judgments, even if at times it meant self-sacrifice. That spirit would enable one to transcend personal gain and profit.

In East Asian culture, a way of looking at the world inherited from Confucianism that is shared throughout the region might be called the "ethos of symbiosis." I am talking about the kind of mentality that favors harmony over opposition, unity over division, "we" over "I." Practically, it is expressed as the idea that human beings should live in harmony with one another and with nature. With such mutual support, the entire community flourishes.

To find and follow a universal Way is one of the most important goals for civilization in the new century.

The Global Economy and Cultural Identity

What interests me as a Buddhist is how we should address the problem of identity. This is because I believe the correct identity base for a true citizen of the world must be one of a global—even cosmic—awareness. Inevitably, a borderless economy results in homogenization and a standardized consumer culture. But the inability of the human spirit to be satisfied with an impersonal identity as a consumer inevitably generates friction, which in turn engenders a kind of particularism.

In his provocatively titled *Jihad vs. McWorld*, Benjamin R. Barber of Rutgers University describes this kind of opposition. According to him, the world today is divided into McWorld, a homogenous global theme park whose driving force is the "universalism of the profit motive (and its accompanying politics of commodities)," [5] and Jihad, whose driving force is the "parochialism of ethnic identity (and its accompanying politics of resentment)." [6]

I have profound doubts about the advisability of using the Islamic term *jihad* as a general synonym for particularism. For the sake of the present argument, however, I would like to adopt Professor Barber's language, because I think it succinctly portrays two contradictory trends in our world.

The demarcations between McWorld and Jihad cannot keep each other out. As long as we look for meaning in our lives, human beings cannot be satisfied to live only in a sterile consumer world, whereas parochialism can never keep out worldwide environmental destruction or halt the tide of the global economy. We are, therefore, virtually fated to endure an identity crisis resulting from our inhabiting a mixture of the two.

More essentially, our world today is dominated by what Buddhism refers to as the "three poisons": greed, anger and foolishness. As long as we continue wandering about in the darkness of ignorance, we cannot discover the light to lead us out of crisis.

World-minded citizens are indispensable to the formation of global democracy. Barber puts great hope in citizens who do not remain shut up in their own private space but actively and independently participate in public affairs. He calls the space in which they participate a "public" and writes: "The creation of a public is the task of civil society. Only there are attitudes likely to emerge that favor democracy and counter the siren song of McWorld. Only there are communities possible that answer the human need for parochial interaction in ways that remain open to inclusion and to cosmopolitan civic sentiments."[7]

The public space, the citizens' field of endeavor, is an

intermediate zone between the government and the private sector. But in the sterile atmosphere of contemporary urban society, developing this kind of vital zone is extremely difficult. Barber offers no clear solutions, though he finds a hint in the lively debate of the early New England town meetings that represent the ideal of American democracy.

If we consider the sources of the American spirit, we see an experimental nation populated by peoples from all over the world. The United States represents global society in miniature and foreshadows, for better or worse, the humanity of tomorrow. As a multiracial nation, the United States faces grave problems. But I am less concerned about the negative aspects of this situation and much more interested in the vitality, energy and creativity generated by the assembly, cooperation and competition of different peoples. In spite of difficulties, the very continued existence of America as a land of youthful energy, freedom, democracy and equality offers great hope that a path to global peace can be found.

The Humanistic State

Discussion of a humanistic economy inevitably leads to questions about the political structure of a humanistic state. In 1974, as I prepared to make my first trip to the Soviet Union, many in Japan questioned my decision. "Why is a Buddhist educator traveling to a nation whose very ideology rejects religion?" they asked. My answer was that I was going "because people are there." Almost three decades later, in a new, post-ideological world, it is even more important that our focus stays on human beings and the right way to live. As Aleksandr Solzhenitsyn so eloquently puts it:

> The structure of the state is secondary to the spirit of human relations. Given human integrity, any honest system is acceptable, but given human rancor and selfishness, even the most sweeping of democracies will become unbearable. If the people themselves lack fairness and honesty, this will come to the surface under any system.[8]

A political system itself guarantees nothing. The countries of Eastern Europe may indeed have overthrown oppressive governments to seize freedom and (they hope) prosperity, yet nothing points the direction to the future. The upheavals, though serving as testimony to the potential of the people's power and as inspiration to oppressed people everywhere, did not necessarily guarantee the fruitful future envisioned by the liberal societies of the Western world, which is itself beset by many problems.

Reality in the advanced capitalist countries of the West hardly permitted delirious shouts of joy. As the war against drugs in the United States indicates, the diseases preying on our souls are far advanced. The nuclear threat may have diminished somewhat, but not a moment can be spared in finding solutions to the ravaging of the environment, the depletion of precious natural resources, the energy crisis and the population explosion. Whereas freedom and wealth ought to be used to enhance the best in humanity, it seems they are working to the contrary. Let us be mindful that freedom and wealth can exact their own severe price.

Even with the end of the Cold War, there has been no increase in the world's sense of security. In recent years, a growing number of military states have given way to democratic forms of government, a trend that brings new hope to many people. But the threat of war remains undiminished because there has been no dominant trend in the world toward disarmament and no progress yet made in ensuring the abolition of war as an institution. There can be no truly humanistic community where war is even a remote possibility.

It follows that the most important step in building such a community is education.

Education Toward a World Community

To ensure that the twenty-first century is a century of hope, our efforts to build a global community without war must be paralleled by the nurturing of human resources, the development of the latent potential of people everywhere. While I applaud the accomplishments of UNESCO, I feel it is time for the entire United Nations to become involved in a wide variety of educational tasks on a global scale. The immensity of the problems that must be resolved on a global scale, including poverty, hunger, the population explosion and the environment, needs to be addressed from a perspective of humankind as a whole. Figures show that approximately nine hundred million people, or thirty percent of the world population over age fifteen, are illiterate. The majority of these people are in Third World countries.

Though military expenditures all over the world rose steadily from the end of World War II, the thawing of East–West relations has reversed that trend and helped reduce them to the lowest point ever in the postwar era. According to a United Nations' report, roughly five percent of the world's annual expenditures on defense would be sufficient to ensure enough food, water, health and education for all the people on the planet during the same period. If that is all that is needed, surely it should be possible to reduce armaments and defense expenditures by five percent.

The problem of education goes far beyond the basic task of learning to read and write. We must also find ways to draw out the latent potential of people who have not yet acquired even the basic know-how of survival and to channel that potential toward the building of a global community.

The problems surrounding education are, of course, very difficult; their remedies call for immense patience and perseverance. Programs to expand education implemented "from above" have often failed for lack of sufficient impetus. If the global education level is to be raised, it will be necessary to provide strong support for internally initiated efforts from the "bottom up."

I believe strongly in the latent power of people. To awaken people to their own power, education is necessary. People need teachers. Today, it seems to me, we are hearing the call for education in global form. In more concrete terms, this course of education must include such currently vital problems as environment, development, peace and human rights.

Education for peace should reveal the cruelty of war, emphasize the threat of nuclear weapons and insist on the importance of arms reduction. Education for development must deal with the eradication of hunger and poverty and should devote attention to establishing a system of economic welfare for the approximately five hundred million people who suffer from malnutrition today and to the two-thirds of the nations that are impoverished. Harmony between humanity and nature should be the theme of education in relation to the environment. It is important to bring the most serious consideration to the extent to which nuclear explosions harm the ecosystem. Learning to respect the dignity of the individual must be the cornerstone of education in relation to human rights. In all four of these essential categories, education must go beyond national boundaries and seek values applicable to all humanity.

Education and Ethnic Exclusivism

Ethnic exclusivism forms a great barrier to our commitment to the global community. At the beginning of the third millennium we find ourselves still face to face with ethnic cleansing, an abominable ghost that has risen from a fifty-year-old grave. Acts of barbarism during the war in Kosovo conjured up the nightmare of the Holocaust, and when we stop to consider that the roots of these atrocities lie in ethnic rivalries that date back hundreds of years, we must question the very notion of progress. The human animal sometimes seems a hopeless creature. I am not alone in feeling this way.

In the last chapter of *Crime and Punishment*, Dostoevsky describes the sensitive young Raskolnikov, who has been banished to Siberia for killing an old money-lending woman. In his dreams, he sees the fierce outbreak of a strange, contagious disease:

> A new kind of trichinae had appeared, microscopic substances that lodged in men's bodies.... Those infected were seized immediately and went mad. Yet people never considered themselves so clever and so unhesitatingly right as these infected ones considered themselves.[9]

Thus people absolutely sure of their own convictions seek out enemies, weaving a pattern of broken alliances as they embark on a road of endless mutual slaughter. In the end, the only ones to be saved from the calamity of the disease are the "pure and the chosen, predestined to begin a new race of men and a new life, to renew and purify the earth...."[10]

This is the nightmare that constantly torments the ailing Raskolnikov.

Today we see people, intoxicated by slogans like "ethnic cleansing," shamelessly shedding human blood. Surely they have been infected by Dostoevsky's "trichinae." They, too, will go on killing one another and show no signs of stopping until humanity is exterminated (and a "new race" created!). Theirs is literally a sickness unto death, an all-devouring, inescapable malaise of the ego.

We must not turn away from the disturbing fact that humanity does not yet possess sufficient immunity against this disease.

The main reason relations among different peoples and cultures degenerate into the kind of atrocity symbolized by ethnic cleansing is to be found in the closed thinking and narrowness that grip people's minds. People of different ethnic groups who managed until only days before to live side by side without particularly overt problems are suddenly at one another's throats, as if prodded and moved only by hatred. It is difficult to believe that the recurrent strife and bloody conflicts we are witnessing today have broken out solely because the restraining frameworks of ideology and authoritarianism were removed. Economic hardship cannot explain it either, though it may have acted as the trigger; if that were the underlying cause, there would be no necessity to resort to killing. We can only conclude that the true cause lies deeper, in a disease of closed-mindedness whose roots are submerged in the history of civilization.

I will address this issue more deeply later, but I believe that the essence of goodness is the aspiration toward unity, while evil directs itself toward division or sundering. The function of evil is ever to create divisions; to cause fissures in the human heart; to sever the bonds among family members, colleagues, friends and acquaintances; to engender enmity between countries as well as ethnic groups; and to destroy the human sense of unity with nature and the universe. Where divisiveness reigns, human beings become isolated and the victims of unhappiness and misery.

A person with a closed heart is one who is shut up within a self-imposed shell of selfishness and complacency. This sad and pointless act of severing self and other bears the hallmark of evil as I have attempted to define it here. This deep-rooted tendency, which has persisted throughout human history, is manifested in a singular way in our time, perhaps a fateful feature of our civilization.

There is no doubt that nationalism, ethnic identity and other much used and abused slogans today have been perfect objects of this easy credulity and fanaticism. This is because concepts like "race" and "ethnicity" are in large part fictitious, and ethnic identifications have typically been artificially constructed by one means or another. This may sound rather extreme, but I believe the circumstances warrant candid words; in a world where ethnic and national identities have become the source of brutal violence, a definitive revision of our understanding of the concepts is critical.

Nationalist sentiments have been intentionally cultivated as an integral part of the process of building modern nation-states; it is a means of forging unity among the citizenry and fostering spiritual bonds. In most cases, its authenticity is highly suspect. Countries like England and France, which are considered models of the modern nation-state, are ethnically and racially more diverse than Japan, for example. It was not so many centuries ago that they were loose federations of smaller tribal groups. Even so, the most rigid of nations *can* reverse its exclusivist impulses.

All People Can Be Victors

A triumph of humanistic community presents itself in South Africa. I have had the opportunity to meet twice with for-mer president Nelson Mandela of South Africa and once with then-Deputy President Frederik de Klerk. In my dis-cussions with both men, I felt strongly that the central ideas driving the move to abolish apartheid were the desire to overcome hatred and distrust and a commitment to dia-logue. Sustained dialogue, in which each party makes every effort to understand the other's position, is the preeminent factor in preventing the slide into violence and chaos and in enabling the splendors of human tolerance to shine through.

In June 1992, Mr. de Klerk expressed these thoughts concerning apartheid: "We desire to create a society in which all people are victors, instead of one consisting of winners and losers who oppose and threaten one another in the pursuit of self-interests."[11]

This determination not to create losers is crucial if we are to resolve the widespread civil strife that plagues our world today. So long as there are even a few losers, people who know the bitter taste of defeat, we can neither hope for a truly stable society nor expect to eliminate completely the seeds of future conflict.

I believe that education is the only tool we have to heal past wounds and build forward-looking societies in which everyone is a victor. At first, education may seem an indirect means of addressing these problems, but I am convinced that it is in fact the most effective means of instilling the spirit of tolerance. Only through learning can we open the spiritual windows of humanity, releasing people from the confines of ethnic or other group-based worldviews. Ethnic identity is deeply rooted in the human unconscious, and it is crucial that it be tempered through unremitting educational efforts that encourage a more open and universal sense of humanity.

South Africa's efforts to create a "rainbow nation" are certain to give hope to other African nations and, by extension, to all who suffer from ethnic divisiveness. South Africa's continuing struggle to champion the spirit of tolerance manifests the kind of philosophy of coexistence that our times demand. The international community should spare no effort to support this unprecedented challenge.

As I observe developments in South Africa, I am reminded that the true source of human happiness lies in the reconciliation and harmonization of different groups, not in their division and conflict. It may be only natural for people to tend to strengthen their association with groups in an attempt to assuage the uneasiness arising from a vacuum of identity. I have come to suspect, however, that national consciousness is largely a fiction half-intentionally created over the course of modern history.

"External Forms" and the Inner Revolution

The Bengali poet Rabindranath Tagore possessed both a delicate sensibility that permitted him to directly grasp the eternal as well as penetrating insight into the nature of human existence. In *The Religion of Man*, he reflected on the nature of ethnic conflicts, what we might call the aporia of human history:

> Our great prophets in all ages did truly realize in themselves the freedom of the soul in their consciousness of the spiritual kinship of man which is universal. And yet human races, owing to their

external geographical condition, developed in their individual isolation a mentality that is obnoxiously selfish.[12]

Tagore forcefully indicts the human brutality and inhumanity that can erupt at any time given the right conditions. He leaves us with the following warning:

> The vastness of the race problem with which we are faced today will either compel us to train ourselves to moral fitness in the place of merely external efficiency, or the complications arising out of it will fetter all our movements and drag us to our death.[13]

Many decades have passed since this cry rose out of the soul of this great poet, and his words shine all the brighter as the regressive phenomena of world history become increasingly evident. It may be possible for opposing groups to reach some agreement concerning "external efficiencies" in the political or economic sphere. Certainly, such understandings are important; but unless we address the issue of "moral fitness" posed by Tagore, hostilities will inevitably break out again at the slightest provocation.

In December 1970, I wrote a long poem dedicated to young people. The reverberations of the fierce student demonstrations that erupted in Japan and other countries in 1968 and 1969 had still not subsided, and only a month before, the outspoken novelist Yukio Mishima shocked the nation with his suicide following traditional rituals. It was, in sum, a time consumed by deep emotions and widespread turmoil. I wrote the poem as a gentle, thoughtful call to young people, including in it my broad vision of the twentieth and twenty-first centuries:

> *What the people long for*
> *to carry them through the twenty-first century*
> *is no reorganization of external forms alone*
> *They desire a sound revolution*
> *carried out within themselves*
> *gradually and in an atmosphere of peace*
> *founded upon the philosophy and beliefs*
> *of each individual*
> *This calls for farsighted judgments*
> *and a profound system of principles*
> *This is what I would name a total revolution*
> *and it is this*
> *we call kosen-rufu.*[14]

The twentieth century was a time of obsessive and reckless pursuit of solutions through social reform, that is, the remodeling of "external forms." Now the primary task we cannot avoid in the twenty-first century is to attend to the revolution within ourselves, what I described as "a sound

revolution carried out within...gradually and in an atmosphere of peace." I entrusted to this poem my strong belief
that the point of departure for everything we attempt from
now on must be the redirection of our primary goal.

In this poem I call on young people to shift the vector of
their youthful energies. Instead of starting with the external, in the belief that changes there would bring about internal change, I made my case for a bold shift to change from
within as the key to changing the world outside. Engineer-
ing this shift is the unavoidable concern we will carry into the
new century. This task has during the past three decades
become the urgent demand of our times.

In that year, 1970, the leftist movement of which the student movement was a part at long last began to show signs
of slackening and declining in response to the disillusion-
ment brought on by the 1968 invasion of Czechoslovakia by
Warsaw Pact troops. Still the urge to remake the world
through social revolution of "external forms" clung on stub-
bornly within the halls of academia. That well-known thesis
of Marxism, though now at its lowest ebb — "consciousness
does not determine existence; rather, existence determines
consciousness" and "consciousness is nothing but the existence one is conscious of" — at that time still held sway
among the leftist camp of opinion leaders.

Amid all the turmoil of the times, I could not help catch-
ing the telltale scent of nihilism and decadence stealing in to

the momentary fervor of anarchy. I felt that I had to appeal to the young for a bold redirection of their thinking and actions.

The following decades witnessed immense tragedy. The century that validated revolution only of "external forms" has been essentially a century of wars and revolutions, and its devastating and cruel toll is now exposed for all to see. The aftermath of the collapse of the Soviet Union and its satellites is a particularly pitiful sight: partly because socialism sought to legitimize social upheaval of "external forms" with theoretical flourishes that distinguished it from the vandalism of the Nazis, and partly because socialism attracted so many young and conscientious idealists indignant at the inherent contradictions of capitalism.

The words of novelist Chingiz Aitmatov from Kyrgystan, with whom I have spoken many times, are unforgettable. He said:

> A piece of fatherly advice: revolution is riot. Young people, put no trust in social revolutions! For nations, people, and society, it is mass sickness, mass violence, and general catastrophe. We Russians have learned this fully. Seek instead democratic reformation as the way to bloodless evolution and the gradual rebuilding of society. Evolution demands more time and patience, more compromises than revolution. It requires the building and cultivating of

happiness, not its forceful establishment. I pray to god that the younger generations will learn from our mistakes![15]

But even the liberalist societies could not rest easy and dismiss the tragedies of socialism's demise as "fires on the opposite shore." The collapse of socialism might be interpreted as evidence of the relative superiority of liberalism and capitalism, and yet conditions in the free societies themselves were not exactly shining with the glow of victory. I believe it must be said that, although liberalism may not have been as extreme in ideological terms as socialism, it was equally obsessed with the revolution of outward forms.

Indeed, as the situation in the liberal democracies in recent years so clearly portrays, we will never arrive at our goal simply by pursuing secular security and external reforms alone. We will end up neglecting the human spirit and cultivation of human character. When that happens, the movement to defend human dignity will degenerate into one that casts down and harms humanity.

The Function of Religion in Community

What is the role of a living religion in today's society? What are the necessary conditions for a world religion? Every religion is called upon to carefully consider and develop answers to such questions.

The inherent role of religion can be defined as taking human hearts that are divided and connecting them through a universal human spirit. Arnold Toynbee addressed that goal when he wrote, "At a time when peoples with very different traditions, faiths and ideals have come into sudden and close contact with one another, the survival of humankind requires that people be willing to live with one another and to accept that there is more than one path to truth and salvation." [16]

This willingness to live and let live is reinforced if we adopt Makiguchi's more proactive stance, that "by benefiting others, we benefit ourselves." This point is the touchstone for the formation of twenty-first century globalism. It is also the tough challenge that no world religion can avoid if it is to be worthy of the name and if it is to fulfill what I see as the true role of faith: providing the profound spiritual energy that will support a mutually beneficial globalism.

Toynbee stressed the importance of accepting that there is more than one path to truth and salvation. Indeed, it is abundantly clear that a stubborn adherence to religious dogma will only exacerbate confrontation and rivalry among peoples, perpetuating humankind's long and bloody history of religious strife and persecution.

Toynbee did not, of course, mean by this that people should not assert their own views of the world, of the universe or of their religious faith. We are free to assert our views, but only as far as this is compatible with the spirit of live and let live, the spirit of tolerance and nonviolence that we of the SGI consider the very heart of humanism. Even as Toynbee held out the possibility that humankind may one day be united in the same faith, he laid down strict guidelines for the propagation of religion, declaring that acceptance of any new faith could only be the result of the free choice of countless individuals.[17]

This idea coincides with what Makiguchi referred to as compliance given "willingly and without reserve."

It is "the religious" that supports, inspires and provides the impetus for people searching for the good and the valuable in their lives; moreover, religious sentiment can offer people a means to access the inner resources that enable them to transcend themselves. This was precisely what Tagore was seeking, and it also constitutes one of the conditions religion must meet if it is to contribute to a more hopeful future.

"Life is struggle," as Johan Huizinger wrote. An incessant struggle between good and evil, between, in the words of Buddhism, the Buddha and the Devil. Freedom and indulgence, democracy and mob-ism, peace and complacency, human rights and self-righteousness are all opposites that are as close to each other as two sides of a coin. To slacken even the slightest in this struggle is to risk succumbing to the other side of that coin.

This is why, now as thirty years ago, I continue to appeal to the young and urge them to practice self-discipline and cultivate their inner selves. Mr. Toda used to tell us, "When young, you ought to experience all sorts of hardships, even at a price," and as I look back on my youth, I can see that maxim is also my unshakable creed. It is the internal revolution that will lay a bridge of hope in the twenty-first century, overcoming all the numerous tragedies of the twentieth century that were caused by our obsession with external reforms.

As we strive for global unity, educational and cultural exchange that transcends the boundaries of religion, race and nationality will become ever more important. Since competition, in its constructive sense, spurs progress, the best way to attain world unity and peace is for nations to compete in what are really character-building activities. Instead of competing to achieve the greatest military strength, for example, countries could vie in the production of strong global citizens.

Our goal should be nothing less than to instill an ethos of worldwide citizenry. As it was with Socrates, by defining ourselves as citizens of the world, we can revitalize in the global community the now almost faded virtues of courage, self-control, devotion, justice, love and friendship, and make them vibrantly pulse in people's hearts.

5
chapter

THE PATH

OF CULTURE

THE PATH
OF CULTURE

As PART OF THE GLOBAL EFFORT to transform the tragic
legacy of the twentieth century, the United Nations declared
2000 the International Year for the Culture of Peace and designated the first decade of the new century (2001–10) the
International Decade for a Culture of Peace and Nonviolence
for the Children of the World. Through these, we have a
unique opportunity to muster the will of the international
community and to initiate action that will transform the age-
old culture of war into a new culture of peace.

How, then, are we to go about the task of creating an
enduring culture of peace? What is really meant by a culture
of peace? Here I propose to discuss the differences between
the culture of war and the culture of peace and attempt to
chart a path from one to the other.

In the time-honored contrast between the sword and the
pen, the latter, of course, is associated with culture and typically evokes an image of peace. But is it really so simple?
When we look at how specific cultural values have been

diffused and how different cultures have encountered one another, it is clear that the process has not always been peaceful. As Arnold Toynbee described it, "the reception of a foreign culture is a painful as well as a hazardous undertaking."[1] As history demonstrates, such encounters are often laden with power struggles and unleash forces that give rise to violence and bloodshed as one culture attempts to subjugate the other. In a sense, the incessant strife we see in the world around us is proof that humanity has yet to transcend destructive modes of intercultural encounter.

I will not attempt here to delve into the difficult question of whether such violence is inherent in the nature of culture or is the result of deliberate distortion and manipulation. Let it suffice to say that culture manifests two contrasting aspects. One resonates with the original sense of the word *culture*— that is, to cultivate—and involves the cultivation of the inner life of human beings and their spiritual elevation. The other is the aggressive, invasive imposition of one people's manners and mores on another, inscribing there a sense of resentment and sowing the seeds of future conflict. In this case, culture serves not the cause of peace but the cause of war.

One classic example of this invasive, aggressive aspect is the cultural imperialism that was intertwined with European colonial policy in the modern era, embellishing it and supplying its justifications. When, with the argument of force, the Europeans invaded and colonized in the nineteenth century, the nations of Asia were living in relative peace and respected one another's cultures. Asia gave wealth, art and culture to Europe, whereas, from the age of the great navigators, Europe used force to victimize Asia. Today, when the limitations of the world's natural resources are evident and when peaceful coexistence is indispensable, Western intellectuals are becoming profoundly aware that peaceful coexistence should replace force and domination.

Cultural Imperialism

The term *cultural imperialism* emerged during the 1960s against the backdrop of the global process of decolonization and through the sub- and counterculture movements in the West, which questioned the legitimacy of received traditions and values. But the reality and experience the term describes date back to the earliest days of European exploration and expansion and are coextensive with the five-hundred-year history of modern colonialism. In essence, it is an ideology that justifies the subjugation and exploitation of other peoples by unilaterally defining them and their cultures as primitive or barbaric.

This is an example of the violent potential of culture in both intent and application. Here culture functioned as the forerunner and as the ideational basis for the war and violence of colonial domination; it served to cover and conceal simpler and rawer forms of collective egoism. Now, at a time when almost all colonies have won independence, it may seem that this veil has been stripped away, and culture is no longer being put to such political uses. The ruptures and struggles that continue to affect every region, however, suggest that this is by no means the case.

Not too long ago, I initiated a dialogue on José Martí, the great nineteenth-century essayist, poet and leader of the struggle for Cuban independence, with Cintio Vitier, president of the Center for José Martí Studies in Havana. These discussions brought back to me the degree to which the strong distrust toward the United States, which Martí noted more than a hundred years ago, remains a firm presence in the minds of the Cuban people today. I believe we cannot dismiss these fears as unjustified.

The Palestinian-born cultural critic Edward Said writes in his book *Culture and Imperialism*, regarded by many as a key work of postcolonial analysis: "[T]he meaning of the imperial past is not totally contained within it, but has entered the reality of hundreds of millions of people, where its existence as shared memory and as a highly conflictual texture of culture, ideology and policy still exercises tremendous force."[2]

As we follow Said's carefully developed and copiously illustrated argument, we discover the depth to which the ideology of cultural imperialism had taken root in the hearts and minds of "decent men and women"—the educated classes of the imperial powers. At the core of Said's argument is his analysis of such literary works as Joseph Conrad's *Heart of Darkness*, Jane Austen's *Mansfield Park* and Rudyard Kipling's

Kim. At the same time, he looks at the underlying attitudes of those intellectual lights—among them de Tocqueville, J.S. Mill, Hegel and Marx—who shaped modern thought and left their imprint on the intellectual life of modernizing Japan, itself a later colonizer that wreaked great suffering on the peoples of Asia. He reveals how these great thinkers, consciously and unconsciously, and with an astonishing freedom from any sense of culpability, supported the goals of cultural imperialism. For example, the French philosopher Ernest Renan could on the one hand write a work such as *The Life of Jesus* and at the same time be a proponent of racial theories rivaling those of the Nazis.

As one final example of these attitudes, here is a statement by Albert Schweitzer, famous for the hospital he operated in equatorial Africa for many decades. "The negro is a child, and with children nothing can be done without the use of authority. We must, therefore, so arrange the circumstances of daily life that my natural authority can find expression. With regard to the negroes, then, I have coined the formula: 'I am your brother, it is true, but your elder brother.'"[3]

It is hardly surprising that Schweitzer's reputation declined rapidly with the rise of independence movements among peoples subjugated by colonialism. And the fact that these words were written with apparent goodwill toward their referents only intensifies our sense of revulsion at the elitist, discriminatory sensibility they reveal.

Cultural Relativism and Globalization

Cultural relativism is an important intellectual legacy of the latter half of the twentieth century. It grew from the pioneering work of cultural anthropologists who sought to balance and redress the arrogant imperialist assumptions that had insinuated themselves into the Western cultural outlook. It is based on the view that specific practices must be understood and appreciated within the context of a culture as a whole; it denies attempts to judge one culture by the values of another or to rank them according to some hierarchical scheme.

There is much to respect in the earnest endeavor to relativize one's own culture and to accord value to traditions that had been looked down upon as savage or primitive. These efforts have done much to ameliorate the noxious effects of cultural imperialism.

I question, however, whether this understanding is adequate as a response to the challenges of globalization — the economic and technological unification of the world. In other words, I fear that an attitude of merely passive recognition or grudging acceptance of other cultures cannot deal with the destructive aspects of culture, which perpetuate a logic of exclusion and confrontation. Unless transformed, these aspects can render culture, in Said's words, "a battleground on which causes expose themselves to the light of day and contend with one another" rather than "a placid realm of Apollonian gentility."[4]

In my discussions with Johan Galtung, the pioneer of peace studies, he lamented the fragility of this kind of cultural relativism for its "tendency to take the form of passive tolerance instead of active attempts to learn from other cultures."[5]

Disputes concerning the universality of human rights between Western countries (in particular, the United States) and countries of the developing world have as their background the attempt to relativize the political culture of the West, from which the modern human rights tradition grew. Attempts on the part of Western countries to criticize the political systems and practices of developing countries are invariably met with countercharges of interference in the domestic affairs of a sovereign state. Equally typical is the rebuttal that the West's attempts to assert the universality of human rights, while ignoring differences in political culture, the history of colonial domination and the resulting disparities in economic development, are at best hypocritical and at worst a continuation into the present of the arrogance of the "Great Powers."

Any attempt to unravel differences and confrontations as complex as these must be grounded in something far more solid than passive acceptance or tolerance. Such attitudes cannot possibly provide the basis for a culture of peace or a new global civilization that will enrich the lives of people far into the third millennium.

Passive cultural relativism does not offer a viable alternative to the highhandedness of cultural imperialism. One necessary aspect of a culture of peace is that it must provide a basis on which a plurality of cultural traditions can creatively interact, learning and appropriating from one another toward the dream of a genuinely inclusive global civilization. Without this kind of overarching goal, we risk being inadequately equipped to meet the challenges of globalization or, worse, of lapsing into a cynical paralysis.

The Promise of Cultural Internationalism

In this connection, let us examine the rich possibilities found in the tradition of cultural internationalism and attempt to broaden and deepen this concept.

Akira Iriye, professor of American history at Harvard University, has written of the cultural internationalism that emerged in the nineteenth century. This movement viewed culture as a vehicle for building cooperative relations across national boundaries and defusing the underlying confrontations propelling the world toward a suicidal arms race. Starting with efforts such as those to promote the exchange of information among scientists and medical practitioners and to standardize systems of measurement, its proponents sought to lay the foundations of peace through educational and cultural exchanges. These networks of exchange survived two global conflicts and were in fact foundational in the postwar efforts that took form in the UNESCO Charter and the Universal Declaration of Human Rights, two key documents that express the common aspirations and conscience of humankind.[6]

In recent years, this same thread has been taken up by the global activities of NGOs and what is known as global civil society. I believe these activities are the first signs of an emerging trend toward what might be termed cultural interpopulism, a movement for cultural interaction in which ordinary citizens are the protagonists. I am convinced this approach will play a key role in the work of building a new culture of peace.

Ryosuke Ohashi, professor of philosophy at the Kyoto Institute of Technology, has pointed out that in intellectual circles in Europe the term *international* has in recent years been largely supplanted by the concept of *intercultural*. Ohashi describes our contemporary world as the intersection of "the vertical axes of a multiplicity of local cultures and the horizontal axes of technology that seeks universality and standardization."[7]

There is a growing, if unspoken, agreement that the realities of such a world can be better grasped by focusing on the deeper issues of cultural identity rather than the more superficial layers of political definitions and concerns.

Indeed, if we are overly entangled in the national dimension, it is easy to lose sight of the fact that national identities are often deliberate constructs created for political ends.

The greatest danger, of course, lies in falling into the trap of viewing them as unchanging entities or essences with an absolute ontological standing.

At the same time, we must recognize that the frameworks of the state — the national level — are not, in the near term at least, likely to disappear and that states will continue to retain an at least functional necessity. We must also confront, however, the reality that there is a deepening crisis of identity that afflicts people everywhere and is driven by what Toynbee termed the "deeper, slower movements of history,"[8] which are not amenable to remedy through purely political means. It is on this profound level that a paradigm shift toward an intercultural perspective is called for.

We must never lose sight of the fact that, however much globalization and communication technology may advance, people still count. The individual — the character of each individual — is decisively the creator and protagonist of culture.

Thus, whether the kinds of popular movements we see today can be successful in generating a culture of peace hinges on several factors. We must first succeed in transcending the excessive attachment to difference that is deeply rooted in the psychology of individuals; and we must conduct dialogue based on our common humanity. I believe that only by confronting this intensely difficult challenge can we transform ourselves and our societies.

Looking back, we see that the twentieth century was an

era in which different ideologies, competing views of justice, vied violently for ascendancy. In particular, we have seen ideologies that were fixated on external differences and distinctions — such as race, class, nationality, custom or cultural practice. These ideologies have claimed that such factors are the key determinants of human happiness and that the obliteration of differences is the most certain path to eliminating the evils and resolving the contradictions of society. The history of the twentieth century is written in the blood of the victims of these deluded ideas.

Social and Political Reform vs. Individual Reform

In June 1945, immediately after the defeat of Nazi Germany by the Allies, Swiss psychologist C.G. Jung addressed these words to "those parts of the body of the German people which have remained sound":

> Where sin is great, grace doth "much more abound." Such a deep experience brings about inner transformation, and this is infinitely more important than political and social reforms which are all of no value in the hands of people who are not at one with themselves. This is a truth which we are forever forgetting....[9]

At the time, Jung's comment attracted little attention. From the perspective of the present, however, it is impossible to suppress astonishment at the historical depth and precision with which this man of wisdom dissected the pathology of our age.

Jung's dismissal of political or social reforms as having "no value" may seem somewhat extreme. We have only to remember, however, the nightmarish misery wrought by those in power who undertook political and social "reforms" without any sense of their need to reform themselves or of the humanity of their victims. Stalin comes to mind. In contrast, in cases where there are prominent individuals who have successfully confronted themselves—for example, Zhou En-lai in the Chinese context or José Martí in Cuba —even the horror of the bloodshed and violence of revolution may be somewhat mitigated and the process of social reform may win support from the citizens over the long term.

The positive aspects of the Chinese Revolution, for example, can nearly all be traced to the extraordinary qualities of Zhou En-lai. Likewise, through my discussions with Cintio Vitier mentioned earlier, I have gained a renewed appreciation for the role that José Martí's legacy has played as the spiritual source and font of the Cuban Revolution.

When we look back over the twentieth century, it is easy to focus exclusively on the negative heritage of that age. But some great achievements toward overcoming social ills must also be acknowledged. One that particularly stands out is the civil rights movement in the United States, which brought about dramatic reforms including the historic Civil Rights Act of 1964 and the bold experiment of affirmative action that followed.

To be maximally effective, legal and structural reforms must be supported by a corresponding revolution in consciousness—the development of the kind of universal humanity that transcends differences from within. It is only when a renewed awareness of our common humanity takes root in individuals throughout society that the dream of genuine equality will be realized. There must, in other words, be a creative synergy between internal—spiritual, introspective—reforms within individuals, and external—legal and institutional—reforms in society. This is one lesson that can be drawn from this dramatic era of change and the sometimes frustrating lack of progress that has followed.

Universal Humanity

There is perhaps no better illustration of the concept of "universal humanity" than the example of Martin Luther King Jr. This finds expression in his words spoken one year before the adoption of the 1964 civil rights legislation. "I have a dream my four little children will one day live in a nation where they will not be judged by the color of their skin but by content of their character."[10]

These stirring words express a profound faith in the power of character. In this sense, they resonate with the teachings of Shakyamuni, who asserted that one is not noble by birth but by actions. José Martí, during the struggle for the independence of his homeland, Cuba, declared his true homeland to be all of humanity. He also asserted that there can be no hatred between races because "there are no races" —that is, race is an artificially constructed concept.

I firmly believe that the key to resolving all forms of conflict among ethnic groups lies in discovering and revealing the kind of universal humanity so powerfully embodied in Dr. King, America's conscience, and José Martí, Cuba's conscience. Any attempt to resolve these issues without treading this challenging path will, I am afraid, be no more than a postponement of the problem.

"Good" and "Evil"

When I referred earlier to a story about Shakyamuni Buddha in which he perceived an invisible arrow piercing people's hearts, I interpreted this as the "arrow" of excessive attachment to difference and asserted that overcoming this kind of attachment is crucial to the creation of peace. I had in mind the special difficulties of resolving inter-ethnic and communal strife. To return to Jung, as he wrote in *The Undiscovered Self*, "If a world wide consciousness could arise that all

division and all antagonism are due to the splitting of opposites in the psyche, then one would really know where to
attack."[11]   Jung is stressing the fact that we must not be
focused solely on that which is external to ourselves. We
must resist the temptation to assign good exclusively to one
side and evil to the other. In fact, we need to reexamine the
very meaning of good and evil.

The external manifestations of good and evil are relative
and transmutable. They only appear absolute and immutable
when the human heart is in thrall to the spell of language
and abstract concepts. To the extent that we can free ourselves from this spell, we can begin to see that good contains
within it evil, and evil contains within it good. Because of
this, even that which is perceived as evil can be transformed
into good through our reaction and response.[12]

From the Buddhist perspective, the true aspect of life is
found in its incessant flux, the way that experiences are generated by the interaction between inner tendencies and
external circumstances. In other words, what we experience
as good and evil are not fixed but depend on our attitude and
response. Good and evil are not unchanging entities. To give
a simple example, anger can function for good when it is
directed at those things that threaten human dignity; in contrast, anger under the sway of self-serving egotism functions
as evil. Thus, anger, which is typically thought of as an evil,
is, in its essence, neutral.

Masters of Language

We can even come to understand the confrontation of good and evil as elements of the semantic network of the human heart, which, mediated through language and symbols, embraces the entire cosmos. From this perspective, even division and confrontation can be appreciated as ultimately indicative of our connectedness to one another and to the universe.

We must not allow ourselves to fall captive to perceived differences. We must be the masters of language and ensure that it always serves the interests of humanity. If we force ourselves to review the nightmares of the twentieth century — the purges, the Holocaust, ethnic cleansing — we will find that all of them have sprung from an environment in which language is manipulated to focus people's minds solely on their differences. By convincing people that these differences are absolute and immutable, the humanity of others is obscured and violence against them legitimized.

In this connection, allow me to quote again from the writings of Chingiz Aitmatov, the gifted author from Kyrgyzstan, who expresses a truly profound insight into the nature of language, the relation between people and their words.

> There are no "homeless" words. Humans are the homes of words, their sovereign masters. Even when people turn to God with the secret desire of

hearing God's voice, it is themselves that they hear
in their own words. Words live within us. They leave
and return to us. They serve us devotedly from the
moment we are born until we die. Words carry the
burden of the world of soul and of the vastness of
the cosmos.[13]

I can keenly appreciate what motivated Aitmatov to examine the function of language with such depth and poignancy.
He lived most of his life under the Soviet regime, in an era
when humans were never the sovereign masters of words.
For people of his generation, words and disembodied concepts were the sovereign masters and humans were forced—
from birth to death—to serve them devotedly.

The work of questioning this inversion was not limited to
literary figures but was the pressing concern of any sensitive
and aware person who lived through that time.

Needless to say, communism was a system entranced by
and obsessed with the concept of a "classless society," one
that sought to overcome difference and distinctions through
purely external, "objective" means. The destructive enchant-
ment of language, its domination of human realities, distorts
the processes of the inner life and causes people to relegate
inner-driven transformation to secondary importance. In this
way, it makes people vulnerable to appeals to the efficacy of
external force—the use of violence. Aitmatov survived a
profound and bitter experience of the kind of ideologically

dominated linguistic culture that accepts or even encourages violence. It is for this reason, I believe, that he was drawn to the Buddhist approach, which rejects violence in all its forms and is unwavering in its commitment to dialogue and the prioritization of human realities.

Nichiren described this as follows:

> To turn from evil is good; to turn from good is evil. Good and evil are not found outside our own hearts and minds. The intrinsic neutrality of life is found in its detachment from good and from evil. Our lives are only to be found in these three properties —good, evil, and the underlying neutrality with respect to good and evil. No reality is to be found other than in our hearts.[14]

This perspective, which focuses on the relativity of good and evil, can help free us from our enthrallment to the conceptualization of good and evil as fixed, external entities, and the corresponding tendency to label others as evil.

Neutral, however, does not mean void or empty. Far from being vacant or void, our lives are manifestations of the cosmic life itself, eternal and overbrimming with the energy of creation.

Nichiren says of the true aspect of life that it "cannot be burned by the fires at the end of a *kalpa*, nor swept away by floods, nor cut by swords or pierced by arrows. It can fit into a mustard seed, and although the mustard seed does not expand, there is no need for life to shrink. It can fill the entire universe. The cosmos is neither too vast nor life too small to fill it."[15]

What is described here is a perfectly clear, pellucid state of life, indestructible and adamantine.

The Buddhist understanding of life can help us translate the ideal of an inner transcendence of difference into the actualities of daily life. In other words, we can achieve a state in which we are no longer caught up in or constrained by our awareness of difference.

In this connection, I am moved to refer to the words of my mentor, Josei Toda, spoken in the period immediately following World War II. Here he described the process by which an individual can transform even the most deeply rooted tendencies, or karma. According to Buddhism, every aspect of who we are—nationality, skin color, family background, personality, gender—is the present result of causes we ourselves made in the past. The law of cause and effect that governs the generation of these differences and distinctions operates consistently throughout past, present and future.

Practicing Nichiren's Buddhism, Toda said, "is the means by which we can transform our karma. When we do this, all intermediary causes and effects disappear, and we can reveal the aspect of the common mortal enlightened since time without beginning."[16]

What Toda refers to as "intermediary" are causes that we have enacted and that generate distinctions on the phenomenal plane — differences of capacity, physical, mental and spiritual differences and the resulting differences in circumstances such as education and occupation. These are, together, the distinctions that make each of us the unique being we are.

When Toda spoke of these intermediary causes and effects "disappearing," he did not mean that the distinctions between people would somehow be obliterated and we would all lapse into sameness or uniformity. This could, of course, never happen. Just as no two people will ever have exactly the same face, differences are an integral, natural and necessary aspect of human society.

For Toda what "disappears" is our attachment to differences, our negative, limiting reactions to differences. This is an example of how a practice of faith can enable the inner transcendence of difference.

The Common Mortal Enlightened Since Time Without Beginning

The goal of embracing Buddhism is to experience within our lives the state that Toda described as "the common mortal enlightened since time without beginning." Nichiren elucidated in his writings the concept of "time without beginning" as meaning to be unadorned, in one's primordial, original state. Thus, when we relinquish all artifice and unleash the natural splendor inherent in our being, we can rise above our differences and see them in perspective, freeing ourselves from excessive attachment to them.

Metaphorically, intermediary causes and effects can be thought of as the stars and moon that grace the night sky and the common mortal enlightened since time without beginning as the sun. When the dawning sun rises in the east, those celestial bodies that had been such a vivid presence through the night immediately fade into seeming nonexistence. They don't, of course, cease to exist, but are simply overwhelmed by the light of the sun, which represents our innate vitality and wisdom. This, I believe, is the function of religious faith and practice. The Buddhist law of causality — that every aspect of who we are is the result of causes we ourselves have made — and the emphasis on an inner transcendence of difference in no way mean that we should passively accept discriminatory practices. The Buddhist idea of inner causation and responsibility should never be allowed to degenerate into the kind of fatalism that causes people to turn a blind eye to real social ills. It is our natural duty to challenge such practices and prejudices and the social structures that give rise to them. Any time religion renders people passive and powerless, it deserves the dishonorable title of "opiate."

On the most basic human level, even if the ideal of a society completely free of all discrimination were to be realized, human differences would persist. The Buddhist terms for the world that we inhabit are all words for difference, distinction and distance, reflecting an understanding that these are the components of experiential reality.

Approach to Differences of Experiential Reality

The crucial question is how we approach these differences.

In my view, the deeper roots of our contemporary problems are to be found in an arbitrary and one-dimensional value system that measures human endeavor against the yardstick of "progress." At a symposium held in January 1997 on challenges of the third millennium, Italian philosopher Umberto Eco offered important insights on this issue.

The symbol of the last two millennia, he said, was an arrow. The concept of time that originated in Judeo-Christian monotheism has been marked by a clear directionality, of which "progress" is one expression. The symbol for the third millennium, he declared, should rather be that of a constellation — a society based on respect for the value of cultural pluralism.[17]

The image of a constellation is apt. It evokes the brilliance of many individual stars. Their grouping creates a beautiful constellation, and yet each star's beauty is unimpaired; on the contrary, the splendor of the night sky lies in their diversity. This image is much like the Buddhist doctrine of dependent origination already described, as symbolized by a vast net sparkling with countless jewels suspended above the palace of Indra. Applying this metaphor to human society, the stars represent individual human beings, the constellation is the culture they collectively produce, and the vast expanse of the sky represents a global community of flourishing diversity.

The teachings of Buddhism also employ the analogy of flowering fruit trees—cherry, plum, pear, etc.—each blossoming and bearing fruit in its unique way to express the value of diversity. Each living thing, in other words, has a distinct character, individuality and purpose in this world. Accordingly, people should develop their own unique capabilities as they work to build a world of cooperation where all people acknowledge both their differences and their fundamental equality, a world where a rich diversity of peoples and cultures is nourished, each enjoying respect and harmony.

A related Buddhist principle is that of giving full and creative expression to the intrinsic individuality of the self without clashing with or preying on the individuality of others. It teaches that the true way of living is found in compassion, learning from one another's differences how to grow and improve ourselves and thereby creating a realm of happiness woven of harmony and coexistence.

It should be noted that respect for diverse cultures does not imply the unconditional acceptance of all cultures and cultural practices. While easy acceptance might succeed in protecting specific groups from the forces of cultural homogenization, if inhuman acts and practices are condoned in the name of culture, the price of preserving such culture, in terms of suffering, will be paid by real human beings.

On the other hand, to give a position of centrality to a particular culture, considering its values absolute and universal, is to create an artificial and unhealthy ranking or hierarchy of cultures. What we should pursue, therefore, is not a world order based on the universalization of certain specific values (as in Francis Fukuyama's *And the End of History*) or one which sees cultures in ceaseless conflict (as in Samuel Huntington's *The Clash of Civilizations and the Remaking of the World Order*). Rather, we must seek the "third path," a global civilization whose core values are tolerance and coexistence. To reach this difficult goal, we must first attempt to identify those values and norms that inform the deepest layers of every culture and are in their essence more similar than different.

The Third Path

Czech President Vaclav Havel spoke of this need in an article that appeared in the Japanese press in 1997. After discussing various aspects of the crisis of the present age, he declares, "A single, all-embracing global civilization has arisen." The only meaningful way to lift humankind out of the recurrent conflict and strife caused by the forces of homogenization is, he argues, "to set upon changing our civilization into one that is multicultural in the real sense of the word, which would enable all to be what they want to be and which would not only try to seek ways toward a tolerant, multicultural coexistence but also lead to a more articulate definition of what relates all people and what will allow, through a shared set of values and norms, their coexistence to be creative." He declares that "the resuscitation of fundamental ethics" is an urgent task.[18]

Even as we pursue the ideal of cultural pluralism, we cannot overlook the existence of those values that are truly universal and which must be protected against the encroachments of relativism. These are not, however, externally imposed norms but values that reside in, and are inherent to, the lives of all people. Religious faith can provide the impetus for the clarification and strengthening of such values, and the capacity to do this is, in my view, the most essential criterion for any world religion of the future.

Clarification and strengthening of universal values should also, of course, be within the province of education.

Dr. David L. Norton, the respected American philosopher who was well versed in Tsunesaburo Makiguchi's educational philosophy, shared his view of the Buddhist model of diversity in a 1991 address:

> For the reorganized world that must come, our responsibility as educators is to cultivate in our students a sensibility of respect and appreciation of

cultures, beliefs and practices that differ from their
own. This can only be done on the basis of the recognition that other cultures, beliefs and practices embody aspects of truth and goodness, as the blossoms
of the cherry tree, the sour plum, the sweet plum
and the pear tree each embody beauty in a distinc-
tive aspect. To achieve this means that our students
must abandon the supposition that the beliefs and
practices with which they are most familiar have a
monopoly on truth and goodness. This supposition
is called parochialism, or narrow-mindedness when
it is the innocent result of ignorance, but it breeds
the aggressive absolutism of the "closed society"
mentality.[19]

Similarly, any real and fundamental change in individuals,
according to Jung, can come only from direct personal interaction.[20] I believe that one of the best ways for students, our
future world citizens, to confront other cultures is through
direct exchange, and that the effort of each individual to pursue dialogue today will lead to a culture of peace and a global
community of harmonious coexistence tomorrow.

At present, in economic terms, the world is roughly
divided into the industrialized North and the developing
South. But this division does not necessarily reflect cultural
superiority and inferiority. Among the developing nations
are those whose cultural achievements rank among the most

important aspects of the heritage of all humanity. In terms not of economy alone but of such things as art and literature, the world is astonishingly diverse and much too complex and rich to be divided simply into North and South. Likewise, we must not confuse East–West political or economic systems with their cultural heritage. Unless this distinction is clear, there is a danger that the basic nature of the cultures involved could be misunderstood and fruitful exchange impeded.

New Standards of Achievement

It is preferable to use standards other than economics to evaluate the achievements of a people. For example, what would we find if we examined nations in terms of musical achievements? In terms of noneconomic aspects of human culture, "developed" nations might appear much less advanced than those regarded as "developing." We would possess a more varied and accurate picture of our green planet and its six billion people if it were examined in light of the art, religion, traditions, lifestyles and psychology of its inhabitants.

Real cultural exchange can bring people together everywhere. Exchange can be like the string of a lute striking harmonious vibrations in the hearts of all. There can be no such harmony, however, without that steadfast mutual recognition of equality. Unilateral cultural intrusions plant the dangerous seed of pride in the transmitter and fill the hearts of the recipients with feelings of inferiority or hatred. Genuine exchange can take place only when people approach one another with an honest sense of mutual respect and appreciation of other cultures.

Everywhere, people speak of their desire for East–West cultural interchange. At no time in history has there been as great a need for a spiritual Silk Road extending all over the globe, transcending national and ideological barriers and binding together peoples at the most basic level. Cultural interactions that are a spontaneous manifestation of the popular will can turn suspicion into trust, convert hostility into understanding, and lead the world away from strife toward lasting peace. Too often history has witnessed the overnight dissolution of agreements made solely on the governmental level. The tragic wars that political failures have brought must not be repeated.

There are those who sincerely believe in the historical reality of national or ethnic hostilities. Such antagonisms do persist, but they are essentially based on delusion. Recently, I read the interesting autobiography of Melina Mercouri, an internationally famous Greek actress who from childhood had considered the Turks to be enemies. When she traveled to Nicosia, on the island of Cyprus, to work on location for a film, she found the city divided into hostile Turkish and Greek quarters separated by checkpoints that she, however, was permitted to cross. She was frequently entrusted with messages or small gifts from Greeks to Turks on the other side of the boundary. As time passed, Turkish people also started asking her to perform similar errands and to take letters and other things to their friends in the Greek zone. Reflecting on this experience, Mercouri said to herself: "I saw that they could be friends.... Greeks and Turks would live together in peace if politicians didn't find it useful to keep animosities alive."[21]

When everyone sees the world this way, we will have built a new spiritual Silk Road joining East and West, North and South, in trust and respect.

The Purpose of Art

To know why culture is so important and is an integrating force among people, we have to understand the purpose of art. Art is the irrepressible expression of human spirituality. So it is now, and so it has always been. Into each of the myriad concrete forms of art is impressed the symbol of ultimate reality. The creation of a work of art essentially takes place within spatial boundaries, but through the process of creating, the soul of the artist seeks union with that ultimate reality, what might be called cosmic life. A living work of art is life itself, born from the dynamic fusion of the self (the microcosm) and the universe (the macrocosm).

Art is to the spirit what bread is to the body; through art we find oneness with a transcendental entity, breathe its rhythm and absorb the energy we need for spiritual renewal.

Art also functions to purify the inner being, to bring the spiritual uplift that Aristotle called catharsis. What is this quality in art that has ordained it to play such an elemental and enduring role in human life? I believe it is the power to integrate, to reveal the wholeness of things. In an early scene of *Faust*, Goethe has Faust rapturously declare, "Into the whole how all things blend, each in the other working, living."[22] If we accept this marvelous statement of the interconnection of all living things, then art becomes the elemental modality through which humans discover their bonds with other humans, humanity with nature, and humanity with the universe.

Whether it is poetry, painting or music, a jewel of artistic expression can stir within us an ineffable impulse that carries us soaring through the empyrean, letting us share the experience with others while confirming its reality. Art's force of integration works in living beings by opening the way for the finite to become infinite, for the specificity of actual experience to assume universal meaning. Religion has always worked through art to affirm identity with the universal, as we can see in the intertwining of art and religious ritual in ancient drama. The English author Jane E. Harrison writes, "It is at the outset one and the same impulse that sends a man to church and to the theatre."[23]

At least in the West, however, the social worth of art has become suspect. A French philosopher once posed this question: "What can literature do to help starving children?"

He was questioning the value of literature that demonstrates no concern for social inequalities in a world where human existence itself is threatened. His criticism underscores the narrowness of the literature of Western European nations, for their literary traditions often shut themselves away in enclosed worlds of their own.

On the other hand, it seems almost natural that the conscientious writers of pre-revolutionary Russia were willing to face the suffering of the people squarely. The intense efforts of these artists to seek true meaning in literature inspired me to devote my life to the quest for peace and cultural creativity.

Russian literature has developed in concert with the shared longing among the people for happiness, freedom and peace. It makes questions of the kind asked by the French philosopher superfluous. The profound understanding of human nature reflected in the work of leading Russian writers is firmly rooted in the people themselves. It is they who have nurtured the growth of the national character and ethos. Russian literature could not have been created apart from the people.

In art and other areas of culture, particularity need not conflict with universality. On the contrary, universal validity may depend precisely on national or ethnic particularity. In times like ours when unity in the world is so urgently needed, the spirit of Russian culture and its deep understanding of humanity must inevitably become an inspirational force for all peoples. This understanding will contribute greatly to the quality of cultural exchange in the twenty-first century.

If people from different cultural traditions are willing to work to build tolerant and enduring links rather than indulge in the temptation to dominate and forcibly influence others, the very nature of culture is such that humanity will be enriched by their interaction, and their differences will engender a renaissance of new values.

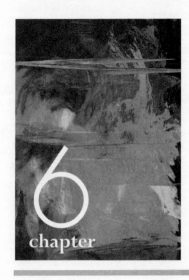

6 chapter

THE PATH

OF NATIONS

 THE PATH
OF NATIONS

WHAT WILL BECOME of nations in the new millennium?

Recent years have witnessed important changes in the nature of relations among states. On the one hand is the trend toward shared sovereignty emerging in the European Community. Juxtaposed to this is the continuing breakup of nation-states in response to demands for autonomy and independence by the peoples that constituted them. Under pressure from both directions, traditional concepts of national sovereignty are undergoing a fundamental rethinking.

The pent-up energies of nationalist and ethnic aspirations have time and again resisted the force of arms and ideology and have often proved powerful enough to expel their oppressors. The strength of indigenous nationalist sentiments derives from the combined power of traditional customs, culture and religion.

Historically, establishing relations of equality and mutual respect among different ethnic groups or races has been much easier said than done. Whether across national boundaries or within a single multiracial nation, the control by one race of another and discrimination and oppression have been the rule, not the exception. But it is a serious error to imagine that the resentment of the oppressed minorities can be held in check indefinitely by the use of force. The disintegration of European and Japanese colonialism and then of the Pax Russo-Americana in recent years can be interpreted as the process through which the hopes and aspirations of oppressed and exploited peoples were brought to the main stage of history. We cannot, and must not, try to reverse this historical current. The rights of all peoples must be protected, and in light of its accomplishments in the past, we must look to the United Nations to take a more active leadership role.

The Dangers of "Universalism"

Leadership, of course, does not mean imposing a universal mode of government. The positive and negative aspects of American-style universalism, for example, are well known: The humanitarianism and idealism that traditionally informed American universalism turned under Truman — and was magnified by Soviet behavior and reactions — into a policy of confrontation. This confrontational ideology, which sought as its professed goal to free people and to maintain their institutions and their integrity against aggressive movements that would impose upon them totalitarian regimes, was a reactionary metamorphosis of idealistic universalism. Thomas

Paine, influential thinker of the American Revolution, wrote that the "cause of America is in a great measure the cause of all humankind," a principle of equality that relates to fully self-confident universalism.[1]

This messianic doctrine cannot be said to have contributed to the establishment of the kind of universal values that transcend races and nations, and in instances such as the Vietnam War and the Iranian Revolution, found itself in direct conflict with the fierce energy of nationalism.

In terms of the gap between internationalism and nationalism, socialism has been beset from the start with even more fundamental contradictions. This is because Marxist–Leninism, putting forward proletarian internationalism as the ultimate value and goal, positions itself at the opposite pole of nationalism.

One of the central themes of the *Communist Manifesto* is that "working men have no country." The authors of the *Manifesto* declare simply that when conflict and exploitation among classes is eliminated, antagonism and exploitation among races or nations will naturally disappear.[2]

In other words, to realize the universal value of the international proletariat, the yearning for national or ethnic self-realization ranks below class consciousness and class-based aspirations.

In fact, however, ever since the Russian Revolution failed to trigger a world revolution — despite the prediction of Lenin and others — this hope that racial and national differences would be submerged in class struggles grew faint with the passing years and has vanished without a trace.

Nationalism and Identity

Let us consider here why nationalism is so much a part of the social fabric and the workings of the human mind. In a nutshell, this problem is closely related to humanity's need for identity. Identity may seem a worn-out subject by now after all the books and articles written on it, but I do not believe the central issue of how we gain the certainty that we are ourselves — the basis of our existence — has been resolved. Rather, as we move from the uniform and standardized civilization of the industrial age to postindustrial society, the identity crisis facing individuals, societies and nations grows more acute. This is one reason the question of national, ethnic or racial identity has also come to the fore.

Whenever I ponder the question of national identity, I am immediately reminded of the tragic last years of Austrian writer Stefan Zweig. As is well known, Zweig, an author of world renown, was forced to flee his homeland by the Nazi German Anschluss of Austria. He ended his own life in Brazil where he had taken refuge. Zweig's memoirs, *Die Welt von Gestern* (The World of Yesterday), depicts in wrenching detail, in a style exuding pain and pathos, the agonized mental state into which he fell when driven out of his homeland. The cruel irony is that Zweig had been a rare cosmopolitan dedicated to the ideal of Europe's spiritual unification. The following passage describes his emotional reaction to the loss of his passport.

> Emigration in itself, whatever the reason, inevitably disturbs the equilibrium. On alien soil one's self-respect tends to diminish, likewise self-assurance and self-confidence; but this cannot be understood until it has been experienced. I have no compunction about admitting that since the day when I had to depend upon identity papers or passports that were indeed alien, I ceased to feel as if I quite belonged to myself. A part of the natural identity with my original and essential ego was destroyed forever.... For all that I had been training my heart for almost half a century to beat as that of a *citoyen du monde* it was useless. On the day I lost my passport I discovered, at the age of fifty-eight, that losing one's native land implies more than parting with a circumscribed area of soil.[3]

Reading this utterly frank and dramatic account of Zweig's identity crisis, one is impressed again with how deeply "nation" and "fatherland" can penetrate the human psyche.

Shuichi Kato, a literary critic and specialist in comparative culture, has pointed out that for an in-depth analysis of fascism, it is not enough to study the works of such authors and intellectuals as Thomas Mann, who fled the Nazis. It is equally important to analyze the thinking of people like Gottfried Benn, who was at first an enthusiastic, but later a reluctant, supporter of the Nazis. Dr. Kato quotes the following passage from Benn:

> Even when things are not going well, this does not alter the fact they are my people. How full of meaning are the words "the German people [*das Volk*]." Everything about me — my spiritual and economic existence, language, life, relationships, my brain — everything is due to the German people.[4]

Though from starkly contrasting perspectives, both Zweig and Benn are talking about the importance of racial and national identity. And it was not just under fascism or Nazism but under Japanese militarism as well that the nation took on an overriding significance for every individual breathing within its framework.

In an increasingly internationalizing world, however, it is no longer productive or meaningful merely to stress the tenacity of racial and national identity or its uniqueness. To continue to do so would be to plunge the world into chaos. As I mentioned earlier, the Pax Russo-Americana, although sustained by enormous quantities of destructive power, did represent a kind of order, and its disintegration does indeed threaten to revive the specter of nationalism all over the

world. This must be avoided at all cost. Neither Zweig nor
Kato is bound, in their arguments, by the narrow framework
of the nation. The gravity of the problem of nationalism
makes all the more pressing the need to overcome it. However difficult the task may be, the establishment of principles and ideals that are at once universal in orientation and
global in scope is an inescapable necessity if we are to cope
successfully with this new century's challenges.

The Need for Self-Determination

In the diverse and interlocking endeavors of people to overcome the current world crises, there does seem to be a common recognition: that the modern nation-state, a progeny of
modern history that ran rampant during the twentieth century, is changing. It might be extreme to describe it as a "hol-
lowing out" of the state, but certainly its presence is less
formidable than it once was.

While the status of sovereign states may have sunk somewhat, it is unreasonable to think that the structural frameworks they provide will easily give way. It would be foolhardy
to quickly establish a world federation or global government
system to replace them; in fact, it could be quite dangerous.
Through the breakup of the former Soviet Union and its
aftermath, the world has learned all too well how, far from
ushering in a new order, the forced dismantling of an existing
framework can lead to anarchy and chaos.

In any case, it would be daydreaming to think that nation-states would simply disappear with the adoption of a world federation. Norman Cousins, known as a vigorous advocate of world federalism, did not think it possible for a unitary world-state to come into being immediately. His idea, rather, was that "there would be clear-cut distinctions between world jurisdiction and national jurisdiction, between the sovereignty that would be pooled in the federation and the sovereignty retained by the nation-states."[5]

Likewise, I do not deny the importance of ethnic or national self-determination. But if we say that the goals of peace and freedom cannot be achieved in its absence, then we are saying that most of the nations and peoples who have not attained statehood in the full sense of the term can never realize these goals. At the same time, we must note that established nation-states have not necessarily succeeded in realizing these goals, either.

It therefore seems clear to me that national self-determination cannot be viewed in absolute terms. Instead, what is needed is a calm and measured look at the factors that prevent the sought-after "fruits" of national self-determination —peace and freedom—from being realized. We must thoroughly examine the circumstances that permit simplistic national rhetoric to take precedence over more complex realities. We must continually strive to remove false trappings and think long and hard about what genuinely constitutes the best interests of the human.

From National to Human Sovereignty

Toward that end, one of the transformations of thought we face in the twenty-first century is what I term a transformation from national to human sovereignty.

Undeniably, sovereign states and issues of national sovereignty have been the prime actors in much of the war and violence of the twentieth century. Modern wars, waged as the legitimate exercise of state sovereignty, have involved entire populations willy-nilly in untold tragedy and suffering.

The League of Nations and later the United Nations, each founded in the bitter aftermath of global conflict, were in a sense attempts to create an overarching system that would restrain and temper state sovereignty. We must acknowledge, however, that this bold project today remains far from the realization of its original aims. The United Nations is laden with a trying array of problems.

If it is to become a true parliament of humanity, the United Nations, I believe, must base itself on the so-called soft power of consensus and agreement reached through dialogue, and that the enhancement of its functions must be accompanied by a shift away from traditional, military-centered conceptualizations of security. To offer a suggestion: Through the creation of a new environment and development security council, the United Nations can, one hopes, be empowered to engage the pressing questions of human security with renewed energy and focus.

In this effort, it is essential that we effect a paradigm shift from national to human sovereignty — an idea expressed powerfully by the words "We the peoples..." with which the U.N. Charter opens. Concretely, we must promote the kind of grass-roots education that will foster world citizens committed to the shared welfare of humanity, and we must foster solidarity among them.

From the viewpoint of Buddhism, the transformation from state to human sovereignty comes down to the question of how to develop the resources of character that can bravely challenge and wisely temper the seemingly overwhelming powers of official authority.

In the course of our dialogues held in the mid 1970s, the British historian Arnold Toynbee defined nationalism as a religion, the worship of the collective power of human communities. This definition applies equally, I feel, to both sovereign states and to the kind of nationalism which, in its more tribal manifestations, is fomenting regional and subnational conflicts throughout the world today. Toynbee further required that any future world religion be capable of countering fanatical nationalism as well as "the evils that are serious present threats to human survival."[6]

In particular, I am unable to forget the profound expectation Toynbee expressed with regard to Buddhism, which he termed "a universal system of laws of life."[7]

Indeed, Buddhism possesses a rich tradition of transcending, and making relative, secular authority through appeals to and reliance on inner moral law.

For example, when Shakyamuni was asked by a Brahmin named Sela to become a king of kings, a chief of men, Shakyamuni replied that he was already a king, a king of the supreme truth.

Equally striking is the drama of Shakyamuni halting the plans of the imperial state of Magadha to exterminate the Vajjian republics (discussed briefly in chapter 3). In the presence of the minister of Magadha, who had come with brazen intent to inform Shakyamuni of the planned invasion, Shakyamuni asked one of his disciples seven questions about the Vajjians. With some elaboration, these are:

1. Do the Vajjians value discussion and dialogue?
2. Do they value cooperation and solidarity?
3. Do they value laws and traditions?
4. Do they respect their elders?
5. Do they respect children and women?
6. Do they respect religion and spirituality?
7. Do they value people of culture and learning, whether they are Vajjian or not? Are they open to such influences from abroad?

The answer to each question was "yes." Shakyamuni then explained to the minister of Magadha that so long as the Vajjians continued to observe these principles, they would prosper and not decline. Thus, he explained, it would be impossible to conquer them.

These are the famous "seven principles preventing decline," the seven guidelines by which communities prosper, expounded by Shakyamuni during his last travels.[8]

It is interesting to note the parallels with contemporary efforts to establish security, not through military might but through the promotion of democracy, social development and human rights.

This incident is also a vivid portrait of Shakyamuni's dignity and stature as a king of the supreme truth addressing secular authority.

It was in this same spirit that Nichiren issued his famous treatise "On Establishing the Correct Teaching for the Peace of the Land" in 1260, directed at the highest authorities in Japan at that time, admonishing them for remaining "deaf to the cries of the people."[9]

From that time, Nichiren's life was a series of unending, often life-threatening persecutions.

He expressed his sense of inner freedom thus: "Even if it seems that, because I was born in the ruler's domain, I follow him in my actions, I will never follow him in my heart."[10]

Elsewhere, "I pray that before anything else I can guide and lead the ruler and those others who persecuted me."[11]

And also, "The occurrence of persecutions should instill a sense of peace and comfort."[12]

Relying on the eternal law within to rise above the sway

of evanescent authority in pursuit of nonviolence and humanity—it is in the course of this grand struggle that one experiences an indestructible life-condition of comfort and security.

I am further confident that these declarations of soaring human dignity will resound strongly and deeply in the hearts of world citizens as they create the global civilization of the twenty-first century.

The United Nations and the "Just Cause"

One requirement for peace among nations is an effective method for resolving opposing notions of justice. As part of the move to revise and strengthen the United Nations, I think it imperative that a commission of wise men and women be set up to map out reform plans. Global in scale, its members should undertake discussion from a genuinely cosmopolitan perspective to deal not only with specific, concrete issues but also with moral, philosophical questions such as "What is justice?"

Crises like the Gulf War involve large questions. For example: What constitutes a just cause to the Arabs? Iraqi President Saddam Hussein linked settlement of the Palestinian question with withdrawal from Kuwait in an attempt to connect the Iraq–Kuwait problem with the whole Arab issue. The United States did not accept this tie-in; that is what ultimately led to the outbreak of war.

There is not space here to discuss the Arab cause in detail, but let me comment briefly on the implications of the expressions "justice" and "the cause." These words possess charismatic power to excite people. Japan, too, before 1945, was aroused by what was called the "eternal cause." Japanese like myself who experienced the war half a century ago cannot hear the word *cause* without wondering what's behind it and recalling that slogan. It is not proper, of course, to equate the Arab cause with the fanatic slogan of Japan's military fascists, but we must be very careful to properly understand its nature, for many lives are being sacrificed in its name.

When I think of justice and causes, the warnings of Austrian jurist Hans Kelsen about the pitfalls of "absolute justice" ring in my ears. He wrote in his book *What is Justice:*

> Absolute justice is an irrational ideal, or what amounts to the same, an illusion — one of the eternal illusions of mankind. From the point of view of rational cognition, there are only interests of human beings and hence conflicts of interests. The solution of these conflicts can be brought about either by satisfying one interest at the expense of another, or by a compromise between the conflicting interests. It is not possible to prove that only one or the other solution is just. Under certain conditions the one, under others the other may be just. If social peace

is supposed to be the ultimate end—but only then—the compromise solution may be just, but the justice of peace is only a relative, and not an absolute, justice.[13]

And earlier in the same essay, he writes: "But the need for absolute justification seems to be stronger than any rational consideration. Hence man tries to attain the satisfaction of this need through religion and metaphysics."[14]

Kelsen asserts that the aspiration for justice is an innate part of human nature, for better or worse. Indeed, it might be said that a person's character is shaped by what he or she considers justice to be.

It is also true, however, that we must forever break away from the topsy-turvy world in which one scale of justice is at loggerheads with another, where humans are turned into the means of struggle between the two and blood is shed for the sake of justice, just as Kelsen warned. Human history is rife with bloody wars fought for precisely this reason. Particularly in societies dominated by an exclusive, monotheistic religion like Christianity, Judaism or Islam, preventing such strife is a serious problem, and many profound thinkers, including St. Augustine and St. Thomas Aquinas, have been arguing since long ago about the nature of a just war.

But does the question of justice and peace really have to be an either-or matter, as Kelsen suggested? I do not think so.

If the yearning for justice is as strong within the human being as Kelsen says, there is sure to be a way to attain true peace through devotion to justice, via a path leading to a higher order of peace and justice. The important thing here is to carefully study the meaning and conditions of justice.

Let us consider the concept of "peace compatible with justice" to replace "war for the sake of justice," as suggested by Professor Emeritus Arthur Kaufmann of the University of Munich. Professor Kaufmann identifies six prerequisites for the attainment of this goal.[15]

First is the principle of equality. Based on recognition of the fundamental sanctity of life, it guarantees dignity equally to all individuals. Among nations, it assures equal opportunity and equal respect in economic and cultural relations. The second prerequisite is the golden rule, as expressed in the Bible: "Do unto others as you would have them do unto you." But Professor Kaufmann translates the rule into an ethical principle and expands on it to include the negative proposition, "Don't do unto others what you would not have them do unto you." The third prerequisite is Kant's famous Categorial Imperative, "Act only on that maxim through which you can, at the same time, will that it should become a universal law." The fourth is the principle of fairness. As in sports, where playing on a level field is the basic rule, in international relations all countries must be entitled to the same advantages and subject to the same disadvantages. The fifth is the principle of responsibility. No action should be taken if consequences might destroy, endanger or degrade people's lives or the environment in which they live, now or in the future. The sixth is the principle of tolerance. Even if your neighbor's thoughts run counter to your own interests, you should respect them.

Space forbids me to go into each of the six prerequisites in detail, but if each country were to adhere to these standards of justice, it might be possible to build a peace compatible with justice, not simply peace as a temporary war-free condition or, in Kelsen's terms, peace as a compromise solution to conflicts of interest. This is the kind of theme that should be deliberated on in the international consultative body discussed earlier.

What would happen if this idea of peace and justice were ignored and if specific religions and ideologies continue to insist that their own definition of justice alone is absolute? Professor Kaufmann quotes Nobel Prize-winning zoologist and ethologist Konrad Lorenz: "The very attempt to keep up the social norms and ceremonies that are believed to represent the highest values is what will lead to religious war, the most horrifying of all wars. And it is [the possibility of] this war that is threatening us today."

Those devoted to religion in the cause of peace and for the sake of humanity must keep these warnings in mind as they go about their work.

The Five Principles of Peace

A measured attitude toward national sovereignty comes to us through Kant, who felt that the sovereign state was not necessarily oppressive and that the interests of the people overlap with those of the state to a considerable extent; he regarded it as a defensive, self-reliant body deserving protection.

This image of the national state persists today and has life-and-death importance for the small and medium nations created in Asia and Africa by the falling away of colonial bonds after World War II. For the people of the Third World, the conscience of all Asian and African peoples is beautifully crystallized in the principles laid down in the first Afro-Asian Conference held in 1954 in Bandung, Indonesia. These five principles of peace are much more than relics of the past:

1. Mutual respect of territorial rights

2. Mutual nonaggression

3. Nonintervention in domestic politics

4. Equality and reciprocity

5. Peaceful coexistence

It is to the credit of the United Nations that, after World War II, the principle of self-determination by the people (the reverse side of the issue of sovereign national state rights) has been advanced in connection with the work of the U.N. Trusteeship Council. In setting limits on state rights, it is essential to make use of such past achievements. This delicate issue, as well as the insistence on voluntary limitation and transfer of sovereign rights, demands a careful, gradual approach.

Similarly, as Richard von Weizsäcker, then president of West Germany, pointed out, citizens of the world should not be rootless; it is roots that give them a consciousness of humanity that is convincing. Tolerance blossoms, he said, not where there is a universal mixture of the rootless but where people are conscious of their national roots. His arguments that awareness of the world does not conflict with patriotism and that the consciousness of being a world citizen is a common self-understanding among Europeans are very important.

Nevertheless, one of the most pressing issues today is to discover a way for ordinary people to break through the great obstacles state and political power continue to present and to open the way to permanent peace.

Purpose of the United Nations

The United Nations from its outset had the two aspects of "the governments" and "the peoples" as the subjects identified in the preamble to its Charter: "we the peoples of the United Nations" and "our respective Governments." But, in reality, the United Nations has always served as an organization of governments and those governments have made all its decisions. The "peoples" have been relegated to the backstage.

I believe the United Nations should enhance the role of people in its organization and operations, because power at the citizen's level is growing rapidly today. Non-governmental organizations, in particular, promise to develop into an effective force for seeking breakthroughs to problems the United Nations has found difficult to solve.

Currently, the relationship between the United Nations and the NGOs, as stipulated in Article 71 of the U.N. Charter, is limited to consultations with the Economic and Social Council. But in reality U.N.–NGO cooperative relations have gone far beyond that. Especially noteworthy is the growing influence of NGOs on interstate diplomacy through their energetic involvement in efforts to cope with global issues, including attendance at U.N.-sponsored conferences on the environment and on arms reduction. These NGO activities—aimed at approaching problems and seeking solutions to global issues for the benefit of the human race rather than individual states—are indispensable.

A democratic system is designed to place a check on government actions and to keep them on the right course. The time is ripe to devise a system to facilitate NGO input directly in the debates at the United Nations. I earnestly hope that through these and other vehicles, the wisdom of the people will be tapped in the effort to revise and strengthen the U.N. system as a reflection of popular will.

One area where NGOs could prove useful is the field of early warning, which is now an important aspect of U.N. activities. In recent years, the United Nations has developed a system designed to collect information and issue early warnings about dangerous crises such as environmental pollution, natural disasters, famine, population movements, epidemics and nuclear accidents. The purpose is to make sure the people concerned are informed and help provide solutions for problems before they reach crisis proportion. The system is an important component of the United Nations' attempts to engage in preventive diplomacy. The NGOs' information-gathering capabilities have been highly commended in the context of this early warning system, and if cooperative relations between NGOs and the United Nations are further developed, the system is sure to be even more effective.

Another dimension of strengthening the United Nations is in creating a mechanism through which the Security Council, the General Assembly and the secretary-general can mobilize all the resources of the various U.N. agencies toward the solution of a given problem. The lack of such an organic, horizontally linked mechanism stands in the way of a vigorous United Nations. As mentioned, an important key to enhancing the overall effectiveness of the United Nations lies in skillfully utilizing the strength of the NGOs. For this reason I propose that, as a provisional measure, some kind of forum be established for regular consultations between the U.N. secretary-general and representatives of the NGOs.

Peace Is the Will of the People

While it is my opinion that the functions of the United Nations must be amplified and reinforced in its work for security and peace, it is up to people themselves to build a world free from strife. The fate of the twenty-first century hinges on whether we give up the idea as impossible or continue to work at the difficult task of achieving true peace. According to archaeologists, humankind has engaged in organized war, meaning clashes between groups, for only about ten thousand of the four million years of human existence on earth. This fact should lead us to the conviction that it is not impossible to realize a human society in which war does not exist.

History's surface is spangled with many distracting events, but these passing phenomena should not bewitch us. Let us instead watch carefully the strong, deep current that determines human history, which is none other than the will of the people. The people of the world are obviously looking forward to the arrival of a world without war, a world of eternal peace.

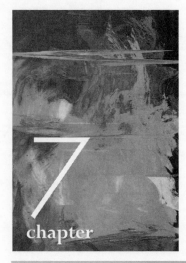

7

chapter

THE PATH OF

GLOBAL AWARENESS

chapter

THE PATH
OF GLOBAL AWARENESS

SOME TIME AGO, astronaut Gerald P. Carr, who served as captain of Skylab 3, shared his thoughts on religion with me:

> As a young Christian man, I conceived of God as a rather fatherly figure, one who was paternal and watched over all of us down here on the Earth. Maybe he pulled a string or two to make things happen and kind of guided our lives. After having seen space, I was impressed by the great universal order of things. Today, I think that order of things in the universe is what we call God, or what other religions call something else. God is the understanding we have that there is order to all things in the universe. It is from this feeling of religion that I believe there is a common universality of all men. I think that is the basis for an understanding of the world community.[1]

Few of us will ever experience viewing our planet from

space; nevertheless, global problems require that we reorient our perspective. We have to come to grips with the realization that the age has ended when we can afford to think of our concerns and responsibilities as limited by national boundary lines drawn from narrow, arbitrary motives.

Globalization has brought to the surface problems that easily cross national borders, such as environmental destruction, poverty and a distressing increase in the numbers of refugees and displaced persons. Likewise, with greater travel, infectious diseases are spreading in new and disturbing patterns. We urgently need measures to deal with these issues. Within the framework of the sovereign–state system, crises have long been defined as territorial issues, and many states therefore have concentrated their efforts on military buildup. But the global issues now confronting us cannot be addressed using conventional approaches. In fact, these problems, when left to fester, cause internal conflicts and wars in many regions.

At the same time, poverty and population growth have a direct, adverse effect on the natural environment as people, struggling to survive, destroy forests through their reckless slash-and-burn agriculture and haphazard search for fuel.

Global Challenges

The three monumental problems confronting humankind— global environmental destruction, population growth and

poverty—are inextricably linked, and we are therefore confronted with the extremely difficult task of finding a simul-
taneous and comprehensive solution.

It goes without saying that effective assistance from industrialized countries is essential if developing countries are to
escape from poverty. Ultimately, however, success depends
on the internal efforts of the poorer countries to develop
themselves, and the key to this lies in education.

Educating people about birth control is one factor necessary to contain population growth. It is important to find a
way to increase general educational opportunities for all people in developing countries. In particular, it has been demonstrated statistically that providing women with educational
opportunities speeds up society's advancement and reduces
the number of children born.

Another prominent problem of our time is the plight of
refugees, whose number has already swelled to some seventeen million people. In addition to ordinary refugees, who
leave their homelands and flee to nearby countries to escape
the ravages of war, we also see a sharp increase in the number of people pouring into industrialized countries to escape
poverty. In addition, victims of ethnic strife wander home-
less within the confines of their own countries. As an NGO
of the United Nations, the SGI recognizes the seriousness of
this international problem and has earnestly undertaken
refugee aid activities.

North–South Imbalances
and Sustainable Development

It would seem we live in an era of pressing choices that demand our immediate response. The choices we make now could well determine the survival of the human race. By their very nature, the global problems confronting us call for the combined efforts of all people, with no distinction between North and South. But in reality, a huge rift has become apparent between the industrialized and developing nations, creating great anxiety. The primary goal of events such as the 1992 Earth Summit is the concrete realization of the concept of sustainable development, which integrates development with protection of the environment. "Development" in this case does not mean the wasteful squandering of natural resources of the past, with its concomitant environmental devastation. Rather, we are groping for a balanced development that ensures environmental preservation. The goal is development that looks directly to the future, that protects the interests of future generations and yet meets the basic needs of the present generation. But the disagreement between the North and the South concerning precisely how sustainable development is to be achieved is far from resolved.

Specifically, there seems to be a rising clamor among developing countries that the unbridled consumerism of the industrialized countries is the primary reason the environment became so degraded in the first place.

It is fantasy to think that the kind of conspicuous consumption of resources by the mass-producing, mass-consuming North could be sustainable much longer. More important, it is very shortly going to be something that global society will no longer condone. A vicious cycle plagues the nations of the South, our close neighbors on this one-and-only earth, linking poverty, population growth and environmental destruction. As many observers have pointed out, the harsh realities of the so-called PPE (poverty, population growth and environment) problem are directly attributable to the North–South disparities that have resulted from the structure of the international economy.

With regard to the polarization of the hemispheres, the 1996 Human Development Report of the U.N. Development Programme warns, "If present trends continue, economic disparities between industrial and developing nations will move from inequitable to inhuman." The report describes the distortions of economic growth under five patterns: (1) jobless growth (growth without an increase in job opportunities); (2) ruthless growth (growth that does nothing to redress the disparity between rich and poor); (3) voiceless growth (growth not accompanied by democratization or the advance of individuals in society); (4) rootless growth (growth that infringes on the ethnic identity of individuals); and (5) futureless growth (growth through wasteful consumption of resources needed by future generations). "In sum," the report says, "development that perpetuates today's inequalities is neither sustainable nor worth sustaining."[2]

Attention at the 1996 World Food Summit focused on the plight of the more than eight hundred million people suffering from starvation or malnutrition in the world, and the Declaration of Rome and a related action plan were adopted aiming to decrease the numbers of the starving by half by the year 2015.

Need for a New Cosmology

Given the scale and scope of the global problems discussed above, it is tempting to posit equally large-scale solutions enforced by a body of enormous transnational power. Although the method may seem roundabout, I suggest, rather, that for the sake of overcoming the identity crises undermining the health of modern humanity we must attempt to discover a new cosmology.

In the European Middle Ages, people lived within the framework of a clearly defined and widely accepted cosmology. This was most eloquently portrayed by Dante's *Divine Comedy*. He imagined the world as consisting of the circles of the Inferno descending to the center of the earth, then the mountain island of Purgatorio, and finally to the celestial

Paradiso, where God dwells. Whatever the merits of the cosmology set out in Dante's masterpiece—and history showed that it could not stand up to scientific verification—it did give answers to the fundamental questions "Who are we? Where did the world come from? Why are we here?" In this way it provided a framework for human identity. By cultivating a sense of divine will at work in times of happiness and unhappiness, pain and pleasure, prosperity and decline, it created a meaningful and well-ordered spiritual hierarchy in which people could live their lives.

The change from the Middle Ages to the modern period, it has been said, represented not a shift from an old to a new cosmology, however, but the abandonment of any cosmology at all. The modern scientific-mechanistic worldview has been built on a refusal even to address these fundamental human concerns and has thus sacrificed any pretense as a cosmology. Unaware of this and determined to remain so, modern humanity mistakes knowledge for wisdom and pleasure for happiness. After having run headlong down the path of modernization, we find ourselves reduced to being mere consumers—the slaves of commodities. It is scarcely surprising, therefore, that the crisis of human identity continues to deepen.

In *Apocalypse*, the British writer D. H. Lawrence called for a renewal of cosmology with an urgency that suggests he foresaw the conditions of our time.

What we want is to destroy our false, inorganic connections, especially those related to money, and re-establish the living organic connections, with the cosmos, the sun and earth, with mankind and nation and family. Start with the sun, and the rest will slowly, slowly happen.[3]

Buddhist Cosmology

At the heart of the SGI movement is the effort to develop a new cosmology and to address the identity crisis head-on. The starting point for this undertaking is the awakening Josei Toda experienced in 1944, while imprisoned for his opposition to Japan's war effort. Having determined on January 1 of that year to read the Lotus Sutra with his whole being, he experienced, through deep prayer, two profound realizations, one in March and one in November.

On the first occasion, he awakened to the reality that what the sutras refer to as the Buddha is nothing other than life itself. On the second, he realized that he too was among the Bodhisattvas of the Earth described in the Lotus Sutra, who symbolize the inherent capacity for enlightened and compassionate action that exists within all people irrespective of education or social status. In the solemn gathering on Eagle Peak during which Shakyamuni expounded the Lotus Sutra, the Bodhisattvas of the Earth receive responsibility to carry on this legacy of compassion into the future regardless of the obstacles they encounter. In other words, Toda realized that the gathering on Eagle Peak and the Bodhisattvas of the Earth were not just a myth but a present reality.

The Lotus Sutra contains many dramatic scenes that have often been dismissed as mere fantasy. Josei Toda's two realizations, especially the second one, accord perfectly with Nichiren's reading of the Lotus Sutra and restore it to full life as a vibrant cosmological panorama. In this connection, those awakenings represent a singular event in the spiritual history of humankind.

While different perhaps from the facts of empirical science, they nonetheless represent experiential psychological facts and, even more important, a universal religious truth. We of the SGI take the drama of cosmological restoration that unfolded in Mr. Toda's heart as our starting point and as the basis of the eternal, immutable identity of the SGI movement.

The essence of Mr. Toda's enlightenment can perhaps be expressed as a profound faith in the infinite worth and potential of human life coupled with a strong determination to awaken people to this.

This cosmology provides answers to fundamental questions inherent in our very humanity. Moreover, it provides a framework—accessible to all—for resolving the identity crisis and transforming chaos into a world where all human beings can find meaning for their existence.

Inner Universalism vs. Social Messianism

At this point, I propose a methodological concept to help guide our search for a new globalism. This is the concept of inner universalism.

Let us first see how this concept can be applied to the individual human being. In his writings, Nichiren said that the inherent dignity of one person serves as an example of all, meaning that all human beings should be regarded as equal. The idea of the absolute equality and the sanctity of all human beings expressed here is the product of the unrelenting inward exploration of life itself as manifested in the individual. Because this view of the human being is internally generated, it leaves no room for distinctions based on such external factors as nationality and race.

By contrast, the kind of universalism that has characterized the confrontational ideologies of the United States and the former Soviet Union is external and transcends the individual. Both liberal democracy and communism are by and large institutional concepts in that they seek to control human beings from outside and/or from above. So while both ideologies go beyond the framework of the nation or the state, they do so in a manner external to the individual.

What, then, are the basic flaws of this type of universalism? The most serious drawback is that, because of its excessively ideological overtones and neglect of the common denominator of humanity, it is quick to divide the world into "good guys" and "bad guys." This particular brand of universalism also easily takes on a messianic character when superpowers are eager to help civilize and enlighten peoples that they consider backward and ignorant. While this missionary spirit can act as a motivating force for creativity and development, it is prone to turn into self-righteousness.

As many intellectual historians have pointed out, messianism has been a prominent feature of American thought ever since the War of Independence. This tradition is an asset when it is informed with the humanitarian idealism of Woodrow Wilson or Franklin D. Roosevelt, but when it joins hands with the confrontational ideology of the Truman Doctrine, it becomes a liability.

In the case of the Soviet Union, messianism takes an even more overt form. In *The World of Yesterday*, Zweig describes what he saw in that country in 1928 when he was invited to participate in the commemorative events marking the centennial of Tolstoy's birth.[4] Presented there is an image of a Russian people brimming with goodwill and naively filled with a burning sense of mission, which derives from the conviction that they are taking part in a historic undertaking for the benefit of all humankind. The specter of Stalinism had not yet raised its ugly head, and the Russians were willing to devote themselves to their national mission. Zweig's observations remind one of Dostoevsky's description of the reaction to a speech he made at festivities in memory of Pushkin:

When I spoke at the end, however, of the universal unity of people, the hall was as though in hysteria. When I concluded—I won't tell you about the uproar, the outcry of rapture: strangers among the audience wept, sobbed, embraced each other and swore to one another to be better, not to hate one another from now on, but instead to love one another.[5]

Placing it in the context of the national aspirations of the Russian people, Nikolai Berdjaev defined communism as a sort of identification of the two messianisms, the messianism of the Russian people and the messianism of the proletariat.[6] This definition aptly applies to the early phase of Soviet communism.

During the postwar phase of Stalinism, this universalistic messianism degenerated into a kind of Great Russian chauvinism, justified in the name of proletarian internationalism. Although Moscow labeled the communist parties in other countries, including those in Eastern Europe, as "fraternal parties," it in fact kept them under its thumb, like a domineering big brother ordering little brothers around.

As a methodological concept, inner universality has a degree of practicality, which in turn dictates a certain pattern of human behavior. Here, universal value is assumed to be inherent in every person, who must develop it within his or her own life. This value, by its very nature, cannot be imposed by force.

The strategy that logically derives from this concept of inner universality is characterized by gradualism, as opposed to radicalism. Whereas radicalism is driven by force, gradualism is propelled by dialogue. The use of force is invariably a product of distrust; dialogue, by contrast, is based on mutual trust and respect.

Whether the God of the Middle Ages or the proletariat of the modern era, so long as the universal value is both external and transcendent, it follows that the greatest good lies in achieving the goals set forth in the interest of that value as quickly as possible. Those who obstinately refuse to support those goals must be forced to change their allegiance by physical or other means of coercion, while those who obstruct their realization must be obliterated by force. What emerges here is a typical form of radicalism. From this point of view, one can understand why the histories of the medieval Christian church and the modern communist movements are filled with instances of force or violence.

A Buddhist View of Time

To help establish such a global or even universal awareness, I suggest the value of reexamining human history on a larger scale and over vaster time spans.

Buddhism speaks of three periods after the death of Shakyamuni Buddha [which modern scholarship locates around 500 B.C.E.]. These are the Former Day of the Law when people embracing his teachings can attain enlightenment; the Middle Day of the Law when Buddhism becomes formalized and less effective; and the Latter Day of the Law when his teachings lose the power to lead people to enlightenment. Each of the first two periods is said to last between five hundred and a thousand years. The Latter Day of the Law is believed to last ten thousand years.

Nichiren writes that "Nam-myoho-renge-kyo [identified by him as the fundamental Law of life] will spread for ten thousand years and more for all eternity."[7] From this long-term perspective, he indicates that his teachings will have the power to awaken people and prevent suffering even in this corrupted Latter Day of the Law and that they will continue to contribute to the welfare of human society into the distant future even ten thousand and more years hence. This is a far-reaching perspective, a great prospect for the future, derived from an extraordinarily profound conviction.

Nichiren's approach can be said to represent the essence of the Buddhist view of history. The three time periods should not be understood in formalistic or categorical terms, nor as a successive, linear flow or advancement of humanity's spiritual history.

It is evident to me that the above-cited passage reflects Nichiren's intense and unflinching struggle in the face of constant official persecution and gives voice to his clear grasp of the deepest undercurrents flowing through human history.

For those who practice Nichiren's Buddhism, his teachings should therefore be read with an attentive view to their deeper significance and an attempt to perceive these undercurrents that flow from past to future. With such a perspective it is possible to identify with his profound compassion for all humanity and to live lives of altruistic service as those Buddhism calls "Bodhisattvas of the Earth."

For this reason, we need to reexamine our understanding of the concept of time. We refer casually to "time" in daily conversation, without considering its implications carefully or being aware of its profundity. Time was a subject of great interest to philosophers such as Martin Heidegger and Henri Bergson. To facilitate my own exposition, I'll draw on Russian philosopher Nikolai Berdjaev's classification of time.

Types of Time

In his essay "History and Eschatology," Berdjaev delineates three classes of time: cosmic, historical and existential.

Cosmic time, which can be thought of as physical time, is measurable by the calendar or clock: one day having twenty-four hours, one year, 365 days and so forth. It is time measured against the regular movements of the solar system.

Historical time is what we think of when we use such expressions as "the twentieth century," "100 B.C.E.," or "the second millennium," referring to junctures along the span of physical time. Even more familiar examples are "today," vaguely considered to be an extension of yesterday, and "tomorrow" as an extension of today.

Berdjaev declares both cosmic and historical time to be "fallen time." This judgment may be easy to accept as far as physical time is concerned, for it is a purely theoretical entity, self-contained and isolated from our subjective involvement. But why historical time?

With regard to historical time, he alludes to a future that "eats up" the present, transforming it into past. This insight merits our careful attention.

In the course of our daily existence, we tend to allow time to slide by, letting tomorrow come as a mere extension of today without purposeful exertion. Such days become expanses of inertia, and we lose sight of the critically important fact that a fruitful tomorrow comes only after a well-lived today.

What Berdjaev calls existential time is experienced when we break free of the fallen time of daily inertia. It is the experience of joy and sense of fulfillment that come from seizing the moment and fulfilling one's innate human mission.

Berdjaev writes that existential time is of such profundity that it cannot be expressed by any mathematical calculation. It is supertemporal time, or time eternally in the present. One moment of existential time can have more meaning, fulfillment and even apparent duration than vast stretches of either of the other two types. It is measured by the intensity of joy or agony experienced in moments when time seems to stand still. One can feel the reality of such time when in the raptures of creative activity or at the moment of one's death.

What is brought to mind by this dazzling leap of enlightenment and revelation in the move from cosmic and historical time to an appreciation of supertemporal, existential time is Tolstoy's novel *The Death of Ivan Ilyich*.

In this story, an ordinary government employee, whose "self-esteem was gratified by the discharge of his official duties; [his] vanity by mixing in good society," lives an ordinary life without any particular vice. Following an accident, however, he is seized by a fatal illness, and in the course of an intense battle with the fear of death, he discovers within himself the light of eternity and true happiness.[8]

With consummate skill, the great novelist portrays the dramatic leap from fallen time to supertemporal time. Ivan Ilyich glimpses the profundity of existential time in the moment of his death, exactly as Berdjaev postulated.

While the cultural milieu that shaped the ideas of both Berdjaev and Tolstoy is within the Christian tradition, these insights can shed important light on the Buddhist understanding of time and history. In his treatise "The Opening of the Eyes," Nichiren quotes a passage from the Contemplation on the Mind-Ground Sutra: "If you want to understand the causes that existed in the past, look at the results as they are manifested in the present. And if you want to understand what results will be manifested in the future, look at the causes that exist in the present."[9]

This passage, too, does not refer to cosmic-time causality, such as the formation of water resulting from the combination of hydrogen and oxygen; or historical-time causality, such as the purported inevitability of the move from capitalism to socialism. Buddhism explains the concept of "the nonsimultaneity of cause and effect" to refer to such linear progressions of causality.

Of most interest to us as human beings, however, are the results that will be manifested in the future. More than any other factor, these are shaped by inner causes in the present moment, that is, by the intensity of our conviction in the plane of what Berdjaev calls the profundity of existential time. This is central to the Buddhist view of time in which the present moment is pivotal — in a sense is everything — and stands in contrast to a historical conceptualization of time in which the future "eats up" the present. Without this pivotal "now," past and future are empty and illusory. Our proper focus must be on ourselves at the present moment. Our actions now should be carried out with intensity, with the realization that the depth of this inner determination is the decisive factor that creates the future and makes history. This view of time and causality is referred to in Buddhism as "the simultaneity of cause and effect."

What Berdjaev described as time eternally in the present or supertemporal time resonates with the Buddhist view, which I describe with the expression "life-time."

Historicism vs. Eternity

The nineteenth and twentieth centuries are characterized by rampant historicism, periods during which humankind turned away, in the name of science, from time eternally in the present or "life-time." In the obsessive pursuit of a blueprint for utopia, nineteenth- and twentieth-century historicism gave itself over to the future that eats up the present, with tragic results. The former Soviet Union became the testing ground for the iron talons of Bolshevism, historicism's most nightmarish manifestation. In my dialogues with former Soviet president Mikhail Gorbachev and Kyrgyzian novelist Chingiz Aitmatov, both men spoke of their deep anguish about those times.

The perspectives of either physical or historical time are also inadequate for a full understanding of Nichiren's confidence that an inner state of vast compassion provides the key to helping people manifest their true, magnificent potential over the next ten thousand years and through all eternity.

Often bitter experiences lead us to awaken to the most profound spiritual truths. The awakening of Josei Toda while in jail for his beliefs also needs to be understood from the viewpoint of existential time. He realized that he was a participant in an eternally present moment, at the ceremony in which the essence of the Buddha's teachings was entrusted to those who would share it with others in the Latter Day of the Law. And he realized that this allegorical ceremony, in which ordinary people (as Bodhisattvas of the Earth) pledge to share with others their understanding of enlightenment to the Mystic Law contained within the Lotus Sutra, continues eternally.

Inner Universalism and Social Action

There is no contradiction between inner universalism and the external, reformist actions of a world citizen. There is an urgent need to educate as many people as possible to become world citizens in order to achieve everlasting peace. The curriculum should cover the most important themes humankind grapples with today — the environment, development, peace and human rights. Each of these topics requires the new point of view of a world citizen, a perspective that goes beyond the confines of national entities. The above four themes are closely related to one another, and the ultimate goal in studying them together is peace for the human race.

Furthermore, I suggest that a World Citizens Charter be created as a base for the education of world citizens. It would be a charter for peace education dealing comprehensively with the four topics. While people's awareness that they belong to the world as a whole is spreading, there are still many conflicts around the globe stemming from racial or religious prejudice.

The preamble of the World Citizens Charter would state that the differences among peoples, in culture, religion and language, are akin to the diversity of species of vegetation rooted in the common soil of the earth, that all the people on earth are world citizens, and that the peace and happiness of humankind will be pursued from this universal point of view.

The existence of world citizens and national independence, of course, are not opposed to each other. In today's world it is fully possible to deepen one's national and cultural identities and to take a broad look at the entire world while working for humanity.

Buddhism calls for participation in the profound spiritual history of humankind, which is possible only through great hardship and struggle; as Berdjaev suggests, by the intensity of joy or agony experienced. It is also a message sent from the depths of history to all cosmic life, the "summons of heroes" that Bergson said is found in a "complete and perfect morality."[10]

Earlier I stressed the necessity of grasping history in larger scales and spans of time. This is because we stand today at an unprecedented turning point in human history. To overcome the various crises facing us, we not only have to cope with the immediate pressing issues, but we also need to probe the depths of time and history in order to obtain a far-reaching vision of the future, centuries or even millennia hence.

Without such a perspective we may be defeated by the daunting array of challenges facing the world today. Courage and hope are essential; we must never lose these vitally human qualities. Each of us must awaken to our unique mission as protagonists in the transformation of history. And we must unite in a shared human struggle to confront and resolve the pressing problems facing our planet.

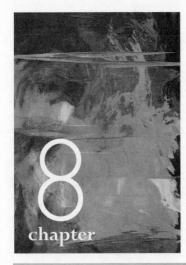

8
chapter

THE PATH OF

DISARMAMENT

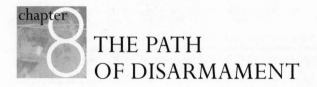

THE PATH
OF DISARMAMENT

On September 8, 1957, Josei Toda, rallying from fatal illness, summoned the strength left to him to appeal to the young and issued his heroic cry for the right to existence for all people of the world:

> We, the citizens of the world, have an inviolable right to live. Anyone who tries to jeopardize this right is a...fiend, a monster....
>
> Even if a country should conquer the world through the use of nuclear weapons, the conquerors must be viewed as devils, as evil incarnate. I believe that it is the mission of all Japanese youth to disseminate this idea throughout the globe.[1]

As is clear from this passage, Toda's idea was an unconditional ban on the use of nuclear arms. To make his will reality, I have stressed the urgency of specific steps to achieve a treaty banning the development, possession and use of nuclear weapons. The declaration against nuclear arms he made — independent of all ideological or national interests and rising above all arguments based on power politics such as nuclear deterrence and limited nuclear war — shines with eternal radiance.

His declaration is imbued with his ardent wish to establish the right to live in peace as a fundamental right for every human being. He earnestly wished that people would not only be kept from the tragedies of nuclear destruction and human sacrifices but also would never again suffer from war. The crystallization of his desire to eliminate all tragedy from the earth embodies a foresight that shares much with the central concepts of human security increasingly called for today. What I would like to stress here is that his declaration — as he expressed it, to "tear away the hidden talons" — was intended to urge those of us of the younger generations to wage an uncompromising fight with the evil part of human life, the invisible enemy responsible for the existence of nuclear arms.

In January 1956, the year before Mr. Toda's antinuclear proclamation was made, John Foster Dulles, then United States secretary of state, announced a "brink of war" policy permitting the limited use of the armament. In May the same year, England conducted nuclear tests. At Bikini, the United States dropped its first hydrogen bomb. Disagreement between the United States and the Soviet Union became increasingly apparent when, in October 1956, President

Dwight D. Eisenhower responded to Soviet Premier Nikolai A. Bulganin's call for a halt to nuclear testing by declaring it an attempt to interfere in the internal affairs of the United States. In May 1957, the Soviet Union conducted a nuclear test. England tested its first hydrogen bomb at Christmas Island. During this period, the United States conducted a series of such tests in Nevada. At the same time, however, the antinuclear movement was gaining impetus. The American chemist and pacifist Linus Pauling collected the signatures of two thousand American scientists on an appeal for the cessation of nuclear tests. The World Conference of Peace issued the Colombo Appeal calling for the immediate and unconditional halt of nuclear tests. In August, the Soviet Union announced successful testing of an intercontinental ballistic missile (ICBM). In December, the United States successfully launched the ICBM Titan. With these developments, the arms race between the two nations gained momentum.

Against this background of increasing tensions between the East and West camps, Josei Toda perceived that nuclear weapons diabolically threaten the human right to continued existence, and he insisted on the importance of carrying this message to the whole world. I sense profound reflection and great wisdom in his decision to make his proclamation forbidding nuclear arms his most important final instruction and behest to youth. Nuclear weapons are absolutely evil; they are of apocalyptic destructiveness and therefore demand different reactions and ways of thinking from conventional weaponry, with which they cannot—must not—be classed.

Surprisingly, however, the lethal and destructive powers of nuclear weapons were at the time thought of as qualitatively similar if quantitatively greater than those of conventional weapons, and few people heeded this call. Even in Japan, the only nation ever to have suffered an atomic bombing, comments about the hydrogen bomb being a "clean" bomb and the importance of nuclear experiments for peace were current. People like Albert Einstein, who said, "The release of atomic power has changed everything except our way of thinking," were in the minority. Inherent in Josei Toda's philosophy was the power to overturn all other ways of thought. This is why, although the peace theories of the ideological left and right have failed to withstand the natural test of time, his proclamation against nuclear arms still shines freshly and brilliantly.

The American journalist Jonathan Schell said the following about the nature of the threat of extinction posed by nuclear arms: "Extinction is more terrible—is the more radical nothingness—because extinction ends death just as surely as it ends birth and life. Death is only death; extinction is the death of death." [2]

The deadly and apocalyptic nature of nuclear weapons produces the awesome concept of the "death of death." The wasteland resulting from a full-scale nuclear conflict would be a place where neither death nor nothingness exists, where there is no meaning of any kind. To prevent such a thing from coming to pass, we must continue in our effort until Toda's philosophy becomes the prevailing spirit of our epoch.

Bertrand Russell, too, called nuclear weapons the absolute evil, and I fully concur. The evil lies not only in their overwhelming power to cause destruction and death but also in the profound distrust emanating from their possession. This distrust has created the so-called cult of deterrence, the belief that nuclear weapons are necessary for protection against nuclear weapons. Trust in nuclear arms is a negation of trust in humanity. The more people trust in arms, the less they trust one another. Ceasing to put their trust in arms is the only way to cultivate mutual trust among peoples.

Renunciation of Nuclear Arms

Some may think that worldwide renunciation of nuclear weapons is an impossible dream, but they must be reminded that it has been only a few decades since U.S. and Soviet representatives seriously talked at the United Nations about the possibility of eliminating all arms. At the Fourteenth U.N. General Assembly in 1959, Soviet Premier Nikita Khrushchev made a speech proposing the elimination of all weapons. The proposal included a detailed program for general and complete disarmament.

In the same year, the Eighty-two-Nation Joint Draft Resolution on General and Complete Disarmament was adopted unanimously at a plenary session of the U.N. General Assembly, calling for total disarmament.

In 1961, the United States and the Soviet Union reached an agreement on the Eight Principles for Disarmament Negotiations, and both countries reported the results of the agreement to the U.N. General Assembly. In September, U.S. President John F. Kennedy made his first speech at the United Nations, presenting a new plan for eliminating arms, known as the Programme for General and Complete Disarmament in a Peaceful World.

In 1962, the two countries submitted the Draft Treaty on General and Complete Disarmament to the newly established Conference of the Eighteen-Nation Committee on Disarmament, and there the drafts became the main topic of deliberation.

What actually developed, however, was an intense arms race between the United States and the Soviet Union. If the world is to enter a new era of arms reduction, it should start afresh, returning to the original spirit of disarmament.

Disarmament Is the Popular Will

One encouraging factor is that a majority of citizens support the abolition of nuclear weapons, even in nuclear-weapon nations like the United States, the United Kingdom and their allies. This was discovered in opinion surveys conducted by NGOs using research agencies in countries participating in the Abolition 2000 campaign. The nuclear-weapon nations cite their citizens' support as part of their justification for the possession of nuclear weapons, but the findings of this research disprove their assertions.

It has been pointed out that nuclear-weapon nations and nations aspiring to join the nuclear-weapons club seek in nuclear weapons a confirmation of their national prestige, in addition to national security. Therefore, a starting point for change is to interrogate these perspectives and the power mentality from which this definition of prestige springs.

In that sense, efforts to fundamentally change people's attitudes exactly meet the demands of our time. As such campaigns gain ever-greater support from the people, a new superpower of trust and solidarity will be born, replacing nuclear-dependent superpowers driven by deterrence and threat.

This common goal — the enactment of a treaty for the prohibition of nuclear weapons — can only be achieved by strengthening the solidarity of citizens.

The obstacles to such a treaty are based on increasingly transparent illusions. If the United States and Russia are no longer enemies, the idea of nuclear deterrence, which has been the dominant justification for nuclear weapons until now, loses all meaning. Therefore, there is no reason to stock-pile thousands of nuclear weapons. We call upon these two countries to completely eliminate their nuclear arsenals because doing so would have great symbolic significance for the cause of worldwide disarmament. If the United States and Russia embark on such a course, which until now has been thought impossible, it is sure to provide great impetus to the process of worldwide disarmament. The path will be cleared for international conferences that include other nuclear powers aimed at the total elimination of nuclear weapons.

Further, the problem of nuclear weapons is not confined to the United States and Russia. We are also confronted with the serious issue of how to prevent global nuclear proliferation. I believe that a new, international organization is needed to deal comprehensively with the increasingly complex problem of nuclear weapons.

One justification for continued nuclear readiness has been the friction between the two Koreas. Peace in Northeast Asia has been my sincere hope, especially in light of the potential that the peninsula possesses. I am also motivated by profound regret for the great suffering Japan's war of aggression caused throughout the region. Recently, relations have been improving steadily toward an environment where fifty years of tension can finally relax and peace can flourish.

To create such an environment, it is essential to foster trust throughout the region. From this standpoint, I called for the creation of a nuclear-free zone in Northeast Asia in my 1997 proposal to the United Nations and for a Northeast Asia Peace Community involving the two Koreas and neighboring countries in my 1999 proposal.

North Korea's nuclear-development program has been the greatest stumbling block to improved relations. Although agreement has been reached between Washington and Pyongyang concerning this issue, strong opposition has surfaced in the U.S. Congress, and many obstacles still lie ahead. Nevertheless, the significance of the agreements reached through dialogue between North and South Korea, and between the United States and North Korea, should not be underestimated.

It is important not to allow ourselves to be swayed emotionally by the vicissitudes of the dialogue process or become pessimistic when agreements are only slowly implemented. A peaceful future can only be created gradually, through the accumulated results of many talks and the slow but steady realization of each agreement.

"Giving Up the Gun"

Another prevalent false assumption is that humankind has never been known to forgo weapons of "superior" technology and that nuclear disarmament is therefore impossible. In his *Giving Up the Gun: Japan's Reversion to the Sword, 1543–1879*, Dartmouth College professor Noel Perrin makes several thought-provoking points.

During the half century from the late sixteenth to the early seventeenth century after the famous warlord Oda

Nobunaga's victory at the battle of Nagashino in 1575, the use of firearms was at its height in Japan. Both in technological quality and in absolute numbers, guns were almost certainly more common in Japan at that time than in any other country in the world. For centuries thereafter, however, throughout the Tokugawa period (1603–1867), the warrior class "chose to give up an advanced military weapon and to return to a more primitive one," in spite of the greater killing power of the former.[3] That is to say, they rejected the rifle and returned to the sword. And from that time onward, the quantity and quality of guns used in Japan dropped sharply.

Professor Perrin gives a number of reasons for this reversal. One of the most arresting is the nature of the sword as a symbol of the human spirit and of morality. In other words, the Japanese based their choices of weapons on what could be called purely internal aesthetic awareness. As a consequence, Edo (what is now modern Tokyo), which had the largest population of any city in the world at the time, gradually and peacefully developed a high level of technology in waterworks, sanitation and transportation systems, while the manufacture of firearms moved from controlled production to such a state of reduction that, by the middle of the nineteenth century, most people had entirely forgotten how to use guns.

Saying "The Japanese did practice selective control,"[4] Perrin evolves two precepts that the Japanese experience proves. "First, a no-growth economy is perfectly compatible with prosperous and civilized life. And second, human beings are less the passive victims of their own knowledge and skills than most people in the West suppose."[5]

The second point offers especially encouraging hope in promoting contemporary disarmament negotiations. Of course, there is no exact analogy between the world's present dilemma about nuclear weapons and the geopolitical conditions that enabled the Tokugawa shogunate to adopt a seclusion policy and to maintain largely peaceful control over the country from the seventeenth to the nineteenth centuries. Nonetheless, making their choice on the basis of internal, spontaneous motives of moral and aesthetic consideration instead of on efficiency of weapon performance alone, the Japanese people of that time could virtually abolish firearms. Their success in this strikes a bitter blow against passive and pessimistic modern views that what is done is done and is irreparable.

Disarmament in Progress

Disarmament has already begun in the modern age. At the end of 1995, I enjoyed discussions on two occasions with Dr. Oscar Arias Sanchez, the former president of Costa Rica and recipient of the Nobel Peace Prize. As we exchanged opinions concerning war and peace, Dr. Arias emphasized that military expenditures should be cut back and the funds spent instead to promote education and culture. In fact, his ideal is to eliminate all armaments worldwide.

After World War II, the Marshall Plan helped rebuild Europe. Dr. Arias contends that a new, global Marshall Plan is now necessary so that resources can be invested in "human development" rather than arms. While it might be easy to dismiss such talk as mere idealism, Dr. Arias's assertions are persuasive in that Costa Rica's constitution, adopted in 1949, succeeded in abolishing that country's armed forces.

Some might say that this achievement was only feasible because Costa Rica is a small country. Nevertheless, the elimination of armaments on a larger scale is not impossible, as evidenced by the abolition of slavery, apartheid and other inhuman institutions when people have finally recognized that they serve no use and bring only harm.

At the urging of Dr. Arias, Costa Rica's neighbor, Panama, revised its constitution in October 1994 to remove the legal basis for its armed forces. Although many problems remain, Haiti, too, has begun to dismantle its army and move in the direction of abolishing its military.

Worldwide, however, there has been little progress so far toward the first stage of nuclear disarmament. More than ten years have passed since the end of the Cold War, but more than thirty thousand nuclear warheads still exist on the face of the earth. No progress has been made either in the ratification of the American and Russian Strategic Arms Reduction Treaty or in negotiations to reduce other kinds of nuclear armament.

Since the indefinite extension of the Nuclear Non-Proliferation Treaty in 1995, the only progress has been the August
1998 decision by the Geneva Conference on Disarmament to
begin negotiating a treaty cutting off production of weapons-
grade fissile materials.

In May 1998, India and Pakistan shocked the international
community by conducting nuclear tests, thereby signaling
their decision to develop their own nuclear arms. In doing
so, they rocked the regime founded on the Comprehensive
Nuclear Test-Ban Treaty and the Nuclear Non-Proliferation
Treaty to its foundations. The international community's fail-
ure to convince India and Pakistan to refrain from such testing exposes the limitations of a one-sided deterrence
doctrine that can be used only by the nuclear weapons states.
There is now a clear danger that other countries may rush to
join the nuclear club.

The United States has recently announced its intention to
use a civilian nuclear energy plant to produce tritium for the
military. Tritium is one of the materials used in nuclear warheads. By taking this step, the United States has abandoned
its once hard-and-fast principle of separating military from
civilian uses of nuclear energy. This, it must be said, demonstrates the arrogance of nuclear-weapon nations and casts
doubts on the sincerity of American disarmament rhetoric.

Nuclear-Free Initiatives

Against this background, in June 1998, eight nonnuclear states—Brazil, Egypt, Ireland, Mexico, New Zealand, Slovenia, South Africa and Sweden—issued a joint declaration calling on the five nuclear powers and nuclear-capable powers like India, Pakistan and Israel, to take disarmament and nonproliferation measures. These same eight nonnuclear countries submitted to the U.N. General Assembly a draft resolution titled "Toward a Nuclear-Weapon-Free World: Time for a New Agenda," which was adopted in December 1998. This resolution makes more concrete proposals than anything yet adopted by the United Nations. For example, it emphasizes the nuclear powers' responsibilities in the area of disarmament and calls for the elimination of all nonstrategic nuclear weapons, the lifting of the state of war-readiness and the issuance of a no-first-use pledge.

The eight countries, often referred to as the New Agenda Coalition, have renounced the possession of nuclear weapons and reliance on the defensive umbrellas of nuclear powers. For this reason, their agenda has earned the support of many other nonnuclear-weapon nations. In particular, Sweden, Brazil and South Africa have the experience of having abandoned nuclear weapons development programs. The coalition's proposal is rooted in the realistic assessment expressed in the words of Fernando Henrique Cardoso, president of Brazil: "We do not want an atomic bomb. It only generates tension and distrust in our region and it would annul the integration process that we are permanently strengthening for the well-being of our people."

Nuclear-free zones have been established in Latin America, the South Pacific, Africa and Southeast Asia, demonstrating that a growing number of regions are renouncing their reliance on nuclear weapons.

Comprehensive Test-Ban Treaty

International society, as we have seen, is very gradually and slowly moving in the direction of disarmament. One important step was the signing of the Comprehensive Nuclear Test-Ban Treaty banning tests and other detonations of nuclear weapons. Despite its adoption by an overwhelming majority of the U.N. General Assembly in September 1996, after an arduous process of deliberation, no clear date has yet been set for the enactment of the CTBT. For it to go into effect, it is required that forty-four nations stipulated as possessing or suspected of possessing nuclear weapons ratify the treaty. As of 2000, only twenty-six have done so. Out of the five permanent members of the Security Council — all nuclear weapon states — only the United Kingdom and France have ratified the Treaty. It has not been signed by India or Pakistan, which both conducted nuclear weapons tests in 1998, or the Democratic People's Republic of Korea; but what greatly set back the prospect of the CTBT entering into force was the rejection of the ratification bill by the United States Senate in October 1999.

During 1999, the U.N. General Assembly adopted a resolution that urges the ratification of the Treaty. But a breakthrough will be almost impossible unless global public opinion in favor of ratification is aroused.

In that sense, it is important to take further steps toward disarmament, particularly in building consensus toward a conscious commitment to disarmament among the nuclear nations. One focus of effort should be the early signing of the "Cutoff Treaty," which would prohibit the production of radioactive material used to manufacture nuclear weapons. Agreement is indispensable to prevent the further proliferation of nuclear weapons that is the basic premise of nuclear disarmament.

Another area of effort is to create the environment for actual reduction of nuclear arms. The Strategic Arms Reduction Treaty negotiations between the United States and Russia are bogged down by the latter's unwillingness to ratify START II. I urge the two countries to break through this prolonged stalemate in talks so that they can carry out its terms. Then, immediately, they must proceed with START III talks to lay the groundwork for the next stage of disarmament negotiations among all the nuclear powers—including the United Kingdom, France and China.

Keys to Disarmament: Trust and Dialogue

At this stage we must ask ourselves, what is the obstacle preventing immediate disarmament? It can only be mistrust. George F. Kennan, former United States ambassador to the Soviet Union and well-known controversialist on the subject of disarmament, explains this distrust by saying: "This is a species of fixation, brewed of many components. There are fears, resentments, national pride, personal pride. There are misreadings of the adversary's intentions — sometimes even the refusal to consider them at all. There is the tendency of national communities to idealize themselves and to dehumanize the opponent. There is the blinkered, narrow vision of the professional military planner, and his tendency to make war inevitable by assuming its inevitability."[6]

This kind of obsession is a horrendous thing.

Exchange of opinions among top leaders is the best way to eliminate the deep-rooted distrust that exists among nations. And, in the long view, removing this distrust can become an indirect cause leading to disarmament and serving as an important key to the achievement of global peace.

Certainly the road to disarmament is long and rocky. Nor does the far-from-successful course of past arms negotiations inspire unmitigated optimism. Nonetheless, the road must be followed. Human hands produced nuclear weapons and weaponry systems, and human hands should be able to reduce and eliminate them. If we stand idle and fail in this, we will rob future generations of their dreams. But even more horrendous, given the total-destruction capabilities of contemporary weapons, we could rob future generations not only of their dreams but also of their very existence.

The Power of People

The time has come for the ordinary people, those who have been tossed about on the waves of war and violence in the twentieth century, to take the leading role in history. They must take the initiative in constructing a new framework for symbiosis. By linking hands in an alliance that transcends national borders, the people can realize a world without war and make our third millennium an era of bright-hued hope.

Indeed, the voices of those who seek a world without nuclear arms have risen to the point where the members of the nuclear club must listen. They can no longer afford to act only with their own interest in mind.

As a Buddhist, I feel compelled to stress the deeper significance of nuclear weapons and the need for their elimination. It is more than a matter of disarmament. It is a question of fundamentally overcoming the worst negative legacy of the twentieth century — distrust, hatred and the debasement of humanity — which was the final outcome of a barbaric, hegemonic struggle among nations. It requires that we face head-on the limitless capacity of the human heart to generate both good and evil, creation and destruction.

The proposals I made to the First, Second and Third Special Sessions of the United Nations General Assembly on Disarmament and the abolition of nuclear weapons represent my desires as a man of religion and express my hope, as leader of the SGI, to protect and support the United Nations.[7]

The abolition of nuclear weapons is more than a question simply of their physical riddance. Even if all nuclear arsenals are removed, a serious question will remain as to how to deal with the knowledge of nuclear arms production that has been acquired by humankind. This is why I say that the only real solution to the issue of nuclear arms is to struggle incessantly against that "evil of life" that threatens the survival of humanity. This is why Josei Toda entrusted younger generations with the task of disseminating the idea of the "dignity of all life" as the overarching ethos of our times.

Counting the Cost

Freezing nuclear weapons at present levels is insufficient for lasting peace. In addition, an international consensus imposing ceilings on all military expenditure, including those on conventional arms, is essential. Ultimately, nothing less than a worldwide renunciation of war will suffice for true human security. To this end, an important factor required for the deinstitutionalization of war is the reduction of the international traffic in conventional arms.

The arms trade intensifies and protracts warfare. Lamentably, far from decreasing, the international arms trade increases year after year. According to "The Military Balance 1998/99," the annual report of the International Institute for Strategic Studies, arms transactions rose by twelve percent in 1997. The increase was especially great in the Middle East and East Asia. Total arms transfers amounted to $34.6 billion in 1997. Other research confirms that areas experiencing regional conflict continue to be the major export market for the arms trade. There is even a thriving market for secondhand weapons in Africa, scene of numerous regional and internal conflicts.

In his April 1998 report "The Causes of Conflict and the Promotion of Durable Peace and Sustainable Development in Africa," U.N. Secretary-General Kofi Annan expressed grave concern about this issue. He requested governments of member states adopt legislation making the violation of a Security Council arms embargo a criminal offense under their national laws. In addition, he requested the Security Council bring to light the covert operations of international arms dealers:

> To profit from warfare and carnage in other countries, to use it to enhance one's own national influence and prestige, to callously sacrifice human life for one's private gain.... The arms trade is evil. Murderous and morally unforgivable, it is an assault

on humanity and human security. It epitomizes the worst that humanity is capable of.

When one country in a region strengthens its military might through arms imports, this heightens regional tensions and instabilities by inciting its neighbors to acquire new weapons systems of their own. Likewise, increasing supplies of arms to the factions in an internal conflict prolong and intensify the fighting.[8]

Breaking this vicious cycle requires a two-pronged approach. The first step is to reduce demand, through efforts to defuse suspicions and build mutual confidence, and the second is to block the supply of weapons flowing into conflict areas.

Ending the Arms Trade

About half of the U.N.-member states now report arms transfers under the U.N. Register of Conventional Arms initiated in 1992. Significantly, although the system is voluntary, the major arms exporters—the five permanent members of the Security Council and Germany—submit reports. As these six countries account for more than eighty-five percent of total arms transfers, their information gives a good idea of the overall situation. To further promote transparency, I propose that a treaty be negotiated

that would expand this system to cover more kinds of
armament and make reporting mandatory for all U.N.-
member states. If implemented, such a treaty would promote world stability by generating trust among member
states and by providing an early-warning system about sudden arms buildups.

I have two other proposals relative to inhibiting the arms
trade. First, we must restrict illicit arms transactions. As is
mentioned in Secretary-General Annan's report, anyone providing arms or covert aid to conflicting parties—especially
if such aid violates a U.N. Security Council arms embargo—
should be strictly punished under national law. We should
also seek consensus within the international community to
expand the competence of the International Criminal Court
to cover the crime of illegal arms trafficking.

Second, major arms-exporting nations should take the initiative in drawing up guidelines to limit the trade.

Many weapons, which have actually served to exacerbate
regional conflicts, have been sold by countries with permanent seats on the Security Council. We have reached the
point where it is essential that restrictions be imposed on
the international arms trade and greater effort made to
strengthen the trend toward disarmament. Talks to this end
among the five permanent members of the Security Council, which started after the Persian Gulf War of 1991, have
broken down. To get them back on track, I suggest that a
G-9 (G-8 plus China) meeting be held to address this topic.

I suggest G-9 is the proper setting since it includes Germany, a major arms exporter, and because it would give Japan and Canada the chance to mediate.

The international community has already adopted treaties and conventions banning such weapons of mass destruction as biological and chemical weapons as well as antipersonnel land mines. As of yet, however, no international disarmament regime is in place for restricting, on the one hand, small arms such as automatic rifles and small-caliber artillery or, on the other end of the scale, nuclear weapons. Some progress has been made. In December 1998, the U.N. General Assembly passed a resolution urging that an international conference to restrict the availability of small arms be held by 2001. Also, the Convention on Chemical Weapons, which had been signed in 1993, finally went into effect in 1997. This convention is thorough enough to be considered a genuine disarmament treaty because it outlaws existing chemical weapons as well as the production of chemical weapons of any kind from here on. It orders the abolition of all chemical weapons, including those that are obsolete or abandoned in other countries' territory, as well as the demolition of facilities for the production of chemical weapons in order to assure the cessation of their manufacture.

The important aspect of this treaty is that it is binding on all signatory nations, thereby resolving the inequities that were an issue with regard to the Nuclear Non-Proliferation Treaty. Also, to prevent violations, the treaty approves a system for inspections of related industrial facilities as well as inspections without prior notice when requests are made. These features make it an extremely good model for future disarmament treaties.

How effective such an epoch-making treaty will prove to be, however, depends on the attitude of the twenty countries that possess or are believed to possess chemical weapons. Particularly regarding the countries that hold most of the world's chemical weapons but have yet to ratify the treaty, international society must unite in urging them to sign the treaty as soon as possible.

I believe that the success of this treaty, with its highly reliable and broad-ranging verification systems, is an extremely important landmark in the movement toward disarmament of other kinds of weapons as well. As each signatory nation conscientiously performs its responsibilities under the treaty and trust is restored through the transparency attained under its verification procedures, the number of signatory nations will increase until it becomes an effective international institution. If success can be achieved even in this single area of chemical weapons, I believe it will have a great impact on endeavors in other areas of disarmament where a consensus has been reached but little real progress made, such as in the case of the Biological Weapons Convention, whose effectiveness, despite having been put into force in 1975, has been drastically lowered because it does not include verification or inspection clauses.

Another such example is the proposed treaty restricting the use of antipersonnel land mines, which saw some progress in 1996. According to studies by the International Red Cross, some eight hundred lives are lost each month and countless people are gravely injured by the one hundred million live land mines that remain strewn about different parts of the world. The vast majority of the victims of land mines are civilians, especially children. The perils of undetonated land mines remain long after the horrors of war are over. I strongly urge that international society move as quickly as possible toward the total abolition of land mines, which imperil the lives and activities of innocent people every day.

Ending Poverty: The Peace Dividend

Reductions in spending on these "conventional" weapons will also allow progress on another essential requirement for a warless world: the eradication of poverty, touched on earlier. Poverty is a key cause of conflict, as it destabilizes societies. Poverty gives rise to conflict, which in turn further aggravates poverty. Severing this vicious cycle would simultaneously lead to the eradication of one of the causes of war and resolve this global injustice. Removing the causes of war and poverty that menace human dignity will enhance enjoyment of human rights.

As I have stated before, we need to shift toward a new

concept of "human security," which centers not on the security of states but on the well-being of people.

Arnold Toynbee once observed that the way to determine whether assistance is directed toward correct long-term goals is to ascertain whether it is designed to link material assistance with spiritual assistance. As Toynbee suggests, assistance up to now has tended to focus on macroeconomic development of the recipient country.

The word *development* has strong utilitarian overtones. In contrast, "human development" encompasses a broader conceptual framework that includes the element of individual commitment. As such, its aim is to draw forth the limitless capacities of citizens. With the United Nations playing a pivotal role, we must strive to create an environment that will encourage and foster the inner potential of each individual, as this constitutes a resource that is both renewable and expandable.

Doing so will make it possible to stop armed conflicts before they begin and to prevent the deadly spiral of violence that brings such misery to humankind. I am convinced that we must take a direct approach to the intractable problem of eradicating poverty as a first step toward correcting the distortions and imbalances that afflict global society.

The strategy of increased military expenditures was used to reduce unemployment and stimulate the economy during the tragic Great Depression of the 1930s. Military spending in World War II is thought to have helped the United

States to overcome those hard times. But increased milita-
rization by one nation always sets up a chain reaction that
other nations follow. As we know only too well, this in turn
can lead to territorial conflicts and even global war.

The myth that growing military expenditures have a positive effect on the economy still persists. The Vietnam War
greatly escalated at a time when the United States' domestic
economy was in recession. But, according to many experts,
the resulting military spending only depressed the American
economy further and caused fiscal deficits.

Authoritative research organizations have shown that
increased military expenditures obstruct wholesome growth
of the world economy.

Global Justice

A further prerequisite to universal disarmament is a system
of global justice. Despite long-standing calls for a permanent
court capable of trying individuals who violate international
laws against genocide, war crimes and crimes against humanity, no such body has been established. In recognition of the
pervasive sense that the international community's response
to the situation in the former Yugoslavia, Rwanda and elsewhere was woefully inadequate, an international conference
was held in Rome in June 1998, where an international
criminal court was proposed.

This court was intended to be a judicial body that would

not only hold individuals accountable for crimes against international humanitarian and human rights law but also provide legal redress to the victims of such crimes. I am eager to see such a court established as a pillar around which the "international law of peace" can be enhanced and elaborated.

Humanitarian issues are not restricted to the scope of any single country. The awareness is finally emerging that they must be dealt with through coordinated international efforts. Attempts to create new systems capable of responding effectively to this need have been viewed by states as attempts to limit and relativize the prerogatives of national sovereignty —which to some extent they inevitably are—and this has prompted protracted resistance to the idea of an international criminal court.

The Role of NGOs

The redoubled wisdom and energy of ordinary citizens are absolutely essential to the work of forging a better future. In this sense, NGOs have an invaluable role to play in providing a voice and a focus for people.

In recent years, we have seen movements in which NGOs have brought the energized efforts of citizens to bear not only on traditional concerns, such as human rights and humanitarian issues; the scope of their activities has expanded to include what might be termed in the broadest sense "human security." This has meant effective NGO activism and advocacy on issues related to arms and security, areas traditionally the exclusive province of the state.

One such achievement is the World Court Project that in June 1997 succeeded in having the legality of nuclear arms reviewed by the International Court of Justice. Similarly, the campaign waged by the International Campaign to Ban Landmines and other NGOs was highly influential throughout the process to draft and adopt the Anti-Personnel Mines Convention in September 1997. These initiatives give great hope and confidence to people around the world who love peace.

The initiative to build a world without nuclear arms and a world without war lies in the hands of every individual. We have to embrace that conviction and be cognizant of our responsibility in that task.

Concerted efforts on the popular level should be encouraged to formulate and then implement constructive plans for a better world; alternatives that will reorient the world toward peace based on the interests of humanity. Expanding such popular solidarity worldwide is the only feasible path toward constructing a world free from nuclear arms and the cataclysm of nuclear war.

The problems confronting humankind are daunting in their depth and complexity. While it may be hard to see where to begin — or how — we must never give in to cynicism or paralysis. We must each initiate action in the direction we believe to be right. We must refuse the temptation to passively accommodate ourselves to present realities and embark upon the challenge of creating a new reality. In addition to these efforts in the public sphere, it is equally essential to create in concrete, tangible ways a culture of peace in daily life.

Peace is not something to be left to others in distant places. It is something we create day to day in our efforts to cultivate care and consideration for others, forging bonds of friendship and trust in our respective communities through our own actions and example.

As we enhance our respect for the sanctity of life and human dignity through our daily behavior and steady efforts toward dialogue, the foundations for a culture of peace will deepen and strengthen, allowing a new global civilization to blossom. When each person is aware and committed, we can prevent society from relapsing into the culture of war and foster and nurture energy toward the creation of a century of peace.

The human spirit is endowed with the ability to transform even the most difficult circumstances, creating value and ever richer meaning. When each person brings this limitless spiritual capacity to full flower, and when ordinary citizens unite in a commitment to positive change, a culture of peace — a century of life — will come into being.

APPENDIX A:
SGI's Initiatives for Peace

Introduction

THE SOKA GAKKAI INTERNATIONAL is a global association of grass-roots organizations that seeks to promote the values of peace and respect for all people. At the heart of the SGI's movement for peace is the ideal of education for global citizenship. Through a wide range of activities, the SGI seeks to foster awareness of the social and environmental responsibilities we all share for the future of our planet. This is education in the broadest sense of the word, and it is not limited to classrooms or to any particular age group.

The SGI promotes cultural exchange and seeks to advance the search for common values, such as tolerance and coexistence, which are present in different forms in all cultures and traditions. These activities are based on the premise that through direct interactions with people from different cultures—whose backgrounds and assumptions about life may differ greatly from our own—we strengthen our sense of common humanity.

The SGI's programs draw inspiration from the humanistic philosophy of Buddhism. Core concepts include:

* The inherent dignity and equality of all human life
* The unity of life and its environment
* The interconnectedness of all beings that makes altruism the only viable path to personal happiness
* The limitless potential of each person to make a difference
* The fundamental right of each person to pursue self-development through a process of self-motivated reform, or "human revolution"

On an organizational level, the SGI — a non-governmental organization with ties to the United Nations — sponsors numerous activities, including exhibitions, cultural exchanges, educational workshops and humanitarian relief efforts worldwide.

And on a personal level, SGI members strive toward the ideal of global citizenship through their Buddhist practice. Buddhism provides a means by which such destructive tendencies as greed, hatred and ignorance can be transformed into altruistic virtues such as courage, wisdom and compassion. A person's triumph over their struggles and challenges, and the resultant unleashing of positive potential, is what is meant by "human revolution." Becoming happy, mastering fear and appreciating how one's life affects others are the objectives of SGI members' Buddhist practice.

The goal of the SGI is a world in which all people enjoy and experience the full dimensions of their dignity as individuals and as inhabitants and citizens of earth.

Peace and Disarmament

The SGI's efforts to promote peace have concentrated on public education projects such as petition drives, book publications, exhibitions and seminars.

Petition Drives

One of the first significant SGI-sponsored petition drives occurred in 1973 when a youth group in Japan launched a national campaign known as "Petition for the Abolition of All Nuclear Weapons and for the Elimination of War." This movement secured ten million signatures in eighteen months, which were presented in January 1975 to then-Secretary-General Kurt Waldheim at U.N. Headquarters in New York.

In 1998, a new generation of youth group members collected more than thirteen million signatures in a three-month period in support of the Abolition 2000 International Petition. Abolition 2000, backed by more than twelve hundred citizen-groups and NGOs worldwide, calls on governments to sign an international treaty committing them to the elimination of nuclear weapons according to a fixed time-table. The SGI's participation in Japan, originated by a young member in Hiroshima whose father had suffered radiation poisoning, spread throughout Japan and then to Italy, the United Kingdom and New Zealand.

Books

With the belief that the memory of the past is a necessary foundation for a better future, the SGI's youth membership has compiled eighty volumes of more than four thousand war experiences from World War II. The SGI's Women's Peace Committee published a twenty-volume work, *In Hope of Peace*, which chronicles the experiences of women who lived through World War II. Since 1980, it has held more than thirty forums appealing for a world free from war and collected more than five thousand anti-war essays written by people who experienced firsthand the ravages of war.

Exhibits

The SGI has developed a series of well-traveled public exhibitions that prove effective in conveying, with impact and immediacy, the horrors of war and nuclear arms. "Nuclear Arms: Threat to Our World" was first presented in 1982 at the United Nations concurrent with the General Assembly's Second Special Session on Disarmament (SSD II) and in cooperation with the U.N. Department of Public Information and the cities of Hiroshima and Nagasaki. The exhibition has since been viewed by 1.2 million people in sixteen countries as part of the World Disarmament Campaign adopted at SSD II. In 1996, the exhibition was updated, and it has been traveling throughout Central and South America. A related exhibition, "War and Peace," has also been touring internationally since 1989. In the United Kingdom, conflict and peace courses have been co-organized by the SGI and the TRANSCEND Peace and Development Network. From these, a new school of "peace journalism" is being developed.

Seminars

A series of lectures, symposiums and seminars have been organized in conjunction with many of the peace-related exhibitions to provide venues for public discussion. Some of these have included:

- The Threat of Nuclear War — Can We Survive?

- Cries for Peace from Ground Zero

- The United Nations in Proper Perspective

- Eyewitness Accounts of the Pacific War

- We and the United Nations

Humanitarian Relief

Buddhist teachings seek to alleviate all forms of suffering. Based on this ethic, SGI members have been actively engaged in various humanitarian activities worldwide.

Fundraising

The SGI organization in Japan since 1973 has raised several million dollars to support the work of the U.N. High Commission for Refugees. It has conducted twenty-two major relief efforts to provide medical care, food, education and other services administered by UNHCR and related organizations.

In response to a request from the United Nations, SGI members in 1993 collected three hundred thousand radios and donated them through the UN Transitional Authority in Cambodia to the people of Cambodia. The radios helped inform the Cambodian public about the first-ever democratic elections to be held in that country. In 1997, SGI members donated funds for the construction of an elementary school in Chheu Teal village in Cambodia.

In 1998, SGI members donated medical equipment to support refugee camps in eastern Nepal. Other recent relief efforts include the allocation of medicine, clothes, clean water and blankets to mudslide victims in Peru; the provision of medicine, clothes and food to flood victims in Argentina; and the donation of funds to support relief supplies for cyclone victims in India, earthquake victims in Bolivia and Iran, and flood victims in China.

In the United Kingdom, working with UNHCR and other organizations, the SGI sponsored concerts in 1997 and 1998 to support War Child, an NGO that provides medical treatment and education for children who are victims of armed conflict. In Malaysia, the SGI sponsored a charity event attended by more than four thousand guests to raise funds for local orphanages, hearing- and sight-impaired treatment centers, and clinics for the treatment of people with kidney or heart diseases. In 1993, SGI members in the UK raised funds to support refugee relief in the former Yugoslavia.

Public Education

In the United States, the SGI-USA's Youth Peace Committee has held a number of conferences to explore social issues such as AIDS and youth violence. A 1998 initiative in Philadelphia brought SGI members together with psychologists, social workers and law enforcement experts to discuss the issue of violence in the local community. In Singapore, the SGI offers monthly courses to the public dealing with such issues as aging and retirement.

Literacy

The SGI also promotes efforts for literacy. In Mauritius, for example, SGI members are supporting UNICEF through volunteer work in literacy training. Additionally, since 1974, the SGI has donated more than four hundred thousand books to 928 schools in the rural areas and remote islands of Japan. It also donated thousands of books to various universities worldwide, and SGI-USA members in 1995 conducted a book drive for African schools that contributed thousands of books to various schools on that continent.

Research

Soka University in 1987 published "An Interdisciplinary Study of the Refugee Problem." The study was conducted with the Independent Commission on International Humanitarian Issues and the U.N. University and submitted to the United Nations.

Human Rights Education

The quest for human rights has been called "a challenge of other-ness" in which individuals develop the courage to acknowledge, respect and appreciate the differences, as well as the similarities, among people.

Grass-roots Activities

On a local level, SGI members seek to bridge these challenges by regularly participating in small group discussions and in cultural exchange activities with peoples of various backgrounds. These grass-roots discussions are the basis of SGI activities worldwide. Along with such community-based events, the SGI sponsors public education activities on regional and national levels to promote an awareness of human rights worldwide.

Exhibitions

Commemorating the forty-fifth anniversary of the adoption of the Universal Declaration of Human Rights, the SGI in

1993 organized the exhibition "Toward a Century of Humanity: An Overview of Human Rights in Today's World." The
display, arranged in cooperation with the U.N. Centre for
Human Rights, is a summary of the evolution of human rights
and present-day challenges to their realization. The exhibition
has been produced in English, French, German, Italian, Por-
tuguese, Spanish, Dutch and Japanese and has been viewed by
more than two hundred thousand people in more than
twenty countries. In 1994, Soka University, in cooperation
with the Simon Wiesenthal Center, an independent United
States organization promoting human rights, premiered in
Japan an exhibition on the Holocaust titled "The Courage to
Remember." Through 1998, it toured forty Japanese cities
and was viewed by more than a million people.

Lecture Series

Lectures and seminars also play a key role in the SGI's human
rights agenda. In Japan, the SGI's Young Women's Peace and
Culture Committee, along with other groups, held a lecture
series titled "Journalism and Human Rights" to explore the
role of the mass media in the promotion of human rights and
the protection of citizens.

The SGI in Italy has sponsored a series of human rights
seminars featuring prominent European scholars and activists,
and Soka University of America hosts a long-running Human
Rights Lecture Series that has over the years featured such
speakers as Rosa Parks, Dith Pran and Morris Dees.

Student Exchanges

Numerous student and youth exchanges are also regularly held in an effort to build peace on a people-to-people basis. Some of these SGI-sponsored activities have included student exchanges between China and Japan; South Korea and Japan; and England and Northern Ireland.

Children's Rights

The SGI-sponsored "World Boys and Girls Art Exhibition," held in cooperation with the U.N. Educational, Scientific and Cultural Organization and various national governments, presents four hundred children's paintings selected from more than one hundred thousand entries from 160 countries. An appeal for peace and friendship from the children of the world, the exhibition has been displayed in countries including Armenia, Azerbaijan, Georgia, Russia, South Africa, Brazil and China. Six other SGI-sponsored exhibitions on children's rights have been held throughout fifty-eight Japanese cities and have been viewed by more than 1.2 million people.

Included among these exhibitions are "Children of the World and UNICEF" and "Treasuring the Future: Children's Rights and Realities," which presents a synopsis of the Convention on the Rights of the Child.

The Soka Gakkai Women's Peace Committee in 1996 issued a "Report on the Education and Dissemination of the Convention on the Rights of the Child," with other NGOs and presented it to the U.N. Committee on the Rights of the Child. The report urges the establishment of a mechanism to promote human rights education and proposes the enactment of legislation to support human rights as an aim and purpose of public education.

Environment

Based on the Buddhist concept of the unity of life and its environment, the SGI sponsors campaigns to educate people about the need to preserve and sensibly coexist with the Earth's biosphere.

Cleanups

On a grass-roots level, SGI members in Japan in 1997 helped in the clean up of badly damaged beaches following an oil spill off of that country's west coast. Also, SGI-Korea members since 1998 have been involved in efforts to support local beautification and cleanup projects throughout South Korea's urban areas.

Research

One of the SGI's affiliated organizations, the Boston Research Center for the 21st Century, has been particularly active in environmental research. A BRC-sponsored conference titled "Religion and Ecology: Forging an Ethic Across Traditions" brought together prominent scholars of religion with specialists in environmental studies. The BRC sponsored a series of Earth Charter consultations across the United States resulting in the publication of two booklets, "Women's Views on the Earth Charter" and "Buddhist Perspectives on the Earth Charter."

Reforestation

In South America, SGI's Amazon Ecological Research Center in Brazil has contributed to the protection of the Amazon River Basin. The Center established two sites in the Amazon for reforestation and native crop cultivation.

The first, at the confluence of the Negro and Solimoes Rivers, is currently raising twenty-five thousand seedlings representing more than fifty native species.

The other site, in Nova Aripuana, is working to transform impoverished, low-productivity agricultural areas into profitable forest through the introduction of progressive managerial and horticultural methods.

Conferences

The Amazon Ecological Research Center, which recently was designated a "natural heritage" by the Brazilian government, also sponsored in 1997 the Amazon Conference on Environment and Sustainable Development in Manaus, Brazil. The exhibition, "The Amazon—Its Environment and Development," was created by the SGI and first presented under the auspices of the 1992 Earth Summit, or U.N. Conference on Environment and Development. It has since toured five countries in South America.

The SGI's conferences and initiatives in support of the environment and environmental studies have included:

- A pre-UNCED conference in the United Kingdom held in cooperation with the Commonwealth Human Ecology Council that helped pave the way for the collaborative NGO–Governmental work-shop at UNCED.

- A 1998 "Respect the Ocean" seminar co-sponsored by the SGI-Australia and the Australian Marine Conservation Society.

- The hosting of numerous public lectures and events to help people learn about the natural environment at Soka University of America's Botanical Research Center and Nursery. The center, established in 1994, currently is home to the largest seed bank of native plant species in the Santa Monica Mountains.

History of the SGI

The SGI today includes more than twelve million members in 163 countries. Its peace, cultural and educational activities are based on the long-standing traditions of Buddhist humanism.

The organization traces its roots back to 1930 when Tsunesaburo Makiguchi (1871–1944) and Josei Toda (1900–58), its first and second presidents, respectively, founded it in Japan as an association of teachers. The group at that time sought to reform the Japanese educational system based on Makiguchi's theory of *soka*, or value-creation, and on the philosophical ideas of the Buddhist teacher Nichiren (1222–82). From its inception, the Soka Gakkai's activities were aimed at empowering ordinary people to develop their unique creative potential. The organization reached a peak membership of three thousand by 1943 before it was disbanded and its leaders imprisoned.

Makiguchi and Toda were outspoken critics of Japan's military government and both were jailed during World War II as "thought criminals" who championed the right to freedom of religious expression. Makiguchi died in prison in 1944 at age seventy-three, refusing to compromise his beliefs.

Toda survived the imprisonment and was released, ill and emaciated, in July 1945, just weeks before Japan's surrender. He set about rebuilding the Soka Gakkai and, with a desire to help individuals who were suffering in the turmoil of postwar society, expanded its mission to include not only education but also the betterment of society as a whole. The organization experienced rapid growth under Toda's stewardship, and in September 1957, shortly before his death,

Toda called on SGI members to work for the elimination and prohibition of nuclear weapons. Toda termed the use of such weapons, for whatever purpose, an impermissible violation of the most fundamental of human rights — that of survival — and condemned the "demonic" nature of their use under any circumstances. This call is seen as the starting point of the Soka Gakkai's peace movement.

Daisaku Ikeda (b. 1928), who had been Toda's close associate, became the third president in 1960 and today serves as president of the Soka Gakkai International — an umbrella association of Soka Gakkai-related organizations worldwide that was established in 1975 to support a growing international membership. Ikeda, a 1982 recipient of the U.N. Peace Medal, has founded various institutions that seek to apply the Soka Gakkai's philosophy to the fields of peace, education and culture. These institutions include the Toda Institute for Global Peace and Policy Research; the Boston Research Center for the 21st Century; the Institute of Oriental Philosophy (in Japan, India, the United Kingdom and Russia); Soka University (in Japan and the United States); the Soka Schools, which run from kindergarten through high school (in Japan, Malaysia, Hong Kong and Singapore); the Tokyo Fuji Art Museum; the Min-On Concert Association; the Victor Hugo House of Literature (France); and others.

Ikeda is also known for meeting frequently with international opinion leaders, educators, cultural figures and common citizens — people from all walks of life — in the pursuit of dialogue toward a peaceful world. Many of these discussions have been published in various languages with the hope that the hard lessons of the twentieth century may be passed down to future generations.

APPENDIX B:
Proposals for Peace

Delivered to the United Nations on January 26 each year in commemoration of SGI Day — the anniversary of the establishment of the Soka Gakkai International. The first peace proposal was presented in 1983, the SGI's eighth anniversary.

1983 New Proposal for Peace and Disarmament

1984 Building a United Movement for a World Without War

1985 New Waves of Peace Toward the Twenty-first Century

1986 Toward a Global Movement For a Lasting World Peace

1987 Spreading The Brilliance of Peace Toward the Century of the People

1988 Cultural Understanding and Disarmament: The Building Blocks of World Peace

1989 Toward a New Globalism

1990 The Triumph of Democracy:
      Toward a Century of Hope

1991 Dawn of the Century of Humanity

1992 A Renaissance of Hope and Harmony

1993 Toward a More Humane World In the Coming
      Century

1994 Light of the Global Spirit: A New Dawn in
      Human History

1995 Peace and Human Security: A Buddhist Perspective
      for the Twenty-first Century

1996 Toward the Third Millennium:
      The Challenge of Global Citizenship

1997 New Horizons of a Global Civilization

1998 Humanity and the New Millennium:
      From Chaos to Cosmos

1999 Toward a Culture of Peace: A Cosmic View

2000 Peace through Dialogue: A Time to Talk —
      Thoughts on a Culture of Peace

ENDNOTES

Chapter 1

1. *See* Tsunesaburo Makiguchi, *Makiguchi Tsunesaburo zenshu* (The Complete Works of Tsunesaburo Makiguchi), vol. 1 (Tokyo: Daisan Bunmeisha, 1983), 14–15.

Chapter 2

1. Benedict de Spinoza, "Of the Best State of a Dominion," *Political Treatise*, ed. R.H.M. Elwes, trans. A.H. Gosset (London: G. Bell & Son, 1883), http://www.constitution.org/bs/poltr_05.htm (November 25, 1998), Constitution Society.
2. Boris Pasternak, *Doctor Zhivago* (New York: Pantheon Books, 1959), 339.
3. Mohandas K. Gandhi, "Who Is A Socialist?" in *The Moral and Political Writings of Mahatma Gandhi: Civilization, Politics, and Religion*, vol. 3, ed. Raghavan Iyer (Clarendon: Oxford, 1986–87), 591–92.
4. Nichiren, *The Writings of Nichiren Daishonin*, ed. and trans. The Gosho Translation Committee (Tokyo: Soka Gakkai, 1999), 1000.

5. Edward McCurdy, trans., *The Notebooks of Leonardo da Vinci* (New York: George Braziler, 1958), 1:90.
6. Nichiren, *The Writings of Nichiren Daishonin*, 997.
7. Ibid., 4.
8. Johann Peter Eckermann, *Conversations with Goethe*, ed. J.K. Moorhead, trans. John Oxenford (London: Everyman's Library, 1972), 100.
9. J. Takakusu, ed., *Nanden Daizokyo*, vol. 23 (Tokyo: Taisho Issaikyo Publishing Society, 1925), 42.
10. J. Takakusu, ed., *Taisho Issaikyo*, vol. 1 (Tokyo: Taisho Issaikyo Publishing Society, 1925), 645c, 15b.
11. Ralph Waldo Emerson, *Essays and Poems of Emerson* (New York: Harcourt, Brace and Company, 1921), 45.
12. Walt Whitman, *Leaves of Grass* (Garden City: Doubleday & Company, 1926), 348.
13. Nichiren, *Nichiren Daishonin gosho zenshu*, ed. Nichiko Hori (Tokyo: Soka Gakkai, 1952), 740.

Chapter 3
1. Nichiren, *Nichiren Daishonin gosho zenshu*, 8.
2. Takakusu, *Nanden Daizokyo*, vol. 24, 358.
3. Josiah Royce, *The Basic Writings of Josiah Royce* (Chicago: The University of Chicago Press, 1969), 2:1122.
4. Takakusu, *Nanden Daizokyo*, vol. 24, 358.
5. John Reed, *Ten Days that Shook the World* (New York: St. Martin's Press, 1997), 21.
6. Gabriel Marcel, *Man Against Mass Society* (Chicago: Henry Regnery Company, 1962), 110–11.
7. Walter Lippmann, *Public Opinion* (New York: The Free Press, 1965), 77.

8. José Ortega y Gasset, *The Revolt of the Masses* (New York: W. W. Norton & Company, 1957), 72.

9. Ibid., 97.

10. Stefan Zweig, *Europäisches Erbe* (European Heritage) (Frankfurt am Main: S. Fischer Verlag, 1960), 286, 287, 288.

11. Michel de Montaigne, *Essays*, trans. J.M. Cohen (London: Penguin Books, 1958), 288.

12. Zweig, *Europäisches Erbe*, 288.

13. Burton Watson, trans., *The Lotus Sutra* (New York: Columbia University Press, 1993), 223.

14. Nichiren, *The Writings of Nichiren Daishonin*, 280.

15. Boutros Boutros-Ghali, "An Agenda for Peace" (New York: United Nations, 1992), 1–2.

Chapter 4

1. Makiguchi, *Makiguchi Tsunesaburo zenshu*, vol. 1, 14–15.

2. Ibid.

3. Ibid.

4. *See* Group of Lisbon, *Limits to Competition* (Boston: MIT Press, 1995).

5. Benjamin R. Barber, *Jihad vs. McWorld* (New York: Ballantine Books, 1996), 219–20.

6. Ibid., 222

7. Ibid., 277

8. Aleksandr Solzhenitsyn, *Rebuilding Russia: Reflections and Tentative Proposals*, trans. Alexis Klimoff (New York: Farrar, Straus and Giroux, 1991), 49.

9. Fyodor Dostoevsky, *Crime and Punishment* (New York: Penguin Books USA, 1968), 524.

10. Ibid., 525

234 FOR THE SAKE OF PEACE

11. "Frederik de Klerk and SGI President Meet," *Seikyo Shimbun*, June 5, 1992, 2.

12. Rabindranath Tagore, *The Religion of Man* (New York: The MacMillan Company, 1931), 154.

13. Ibid., 156.

14. Daisaku Ikeda, "Song of Youth," *Songs From My Heart* (New York: Weatherhill, 1997), 21.

15. Daisaku Ikeda and Chingiz Aitmatov, *Oinaru tamashii no uta*, vol. 1 (Poems of the Great Spirit), trans. Richard L. Gage (Tokyo: Ushio Shuppansha, 1995), 81.

16. Arnold J. Toynbee, "Hiseiyo Bunmei no Shorai" (The Future of Non-Western Civilizations), *Asahi Shimbun*, January 6, 1957.

17. Ibid.

Chapter 5

1. Arnold J. Toynbee, *The World and the West* (London: Oxford University Press, 1953), 81.

2. Edward W. Said, *Culture and Imperialism* (New York: Vintage Books, 1994), 12.

3. Albert Schweitzer, On *the Edge of the Primeval Forest: The Experiences and Observations of a Doctor in Equatorial Africa*, Fontana Edition (London and Glasgow: A. & C. Black Limited, 1956), 96.

4. Said, *Culture and Imperialism*, xiii.

5. Johan Galtung and Daisaku Ikeda, *Choose Peace*, trans. and ed. Richard Gage (East Haven, CT: Pluto Press, 1995), 127.

6. *See* Akira Iriye, *Cultural Internationalism and the World Order* (Baltimore: Johns Hopkins University Press, 1997).

7. Ryosuke Ohashi, *Uchinaru ikoku sotonaru Nihon kasoku suru interculture sekai* (The Foreign Country Within, the Japan Without: The Increasingly Intercultural World) (Tokyo: Jinbunshoin, 1999).

8. Arnold J. Toynbee, *Civilization on Trial* (New York: Oxford Press, 1948), 213.

9. C.G. Jung, "After the Catastrophe," *Essays on Contemporary Events*, trans. Elizabeth Welsh (London: Kegan Paul, 1947), 71.

10. Martin Luther King Jr., "I Have a Dream," *A Testament of Hope: The Essential Writings and Speeches of Martin Luther King Jr.*, ed. James M. Washington, First Harper Collins Paperback Edition (San Francisco: Harper San Francisco, 1991), 219.

11. C.G. Jung, *The Undiscovered Self*, trans. R.F.C. Hull (Boston: Little, Brown and Company, 1958), 101.

12. Ibid., 5–15.

13. Ikeda and Aitmatov, *Oinaru tamashii no uta*, vol. 1, 1.

14. Nichiren, *Nichiren Daishonin gosho zenshu*, 563.

15. Ibid.

16. Josei Toda, speech delivered at Kanda Education Center, Tokyo, October 19, 1947.

17. Umberto Eco, speech delivered on January 23, 1997, at Fondación Valencia Tercer Milenia; as quoted in Eiji Hattori, "*3000 nenki o miru 'sekaijin' ga uttaeru mono*" (Cosmopolitan Appeals for the Third Millennium), Ronza (May 1997).

18. Vaclav Havel, "Insights into the World, Uniting Responsibility for the World," *Daily Yomiuri*, January 27, 1997, 6.

19. Dr. David L. Norton, "Human Education for World Citizenship," speech delivered to the education division of the Soka Gakkai in Osaka, Japan, October 22, 1991.

20. Jung, *The Undiscovered Self*, 40–41.

21. Melina Mercouri, *I Was Born Greek* (Garden City, NY: Doubleday & Co., 1971), 162.

22. J.W. Goethe, *Faust, A Tragedy*, trans. Bayard Taylor (New York: the Modern Library, 1967), 17–18.

23. Jane Ellen Harrison, *Ancient Art and Ritual* (Oxford: Oxford University Press, 1951), 9.

Chapter 6

1. Thomas Paine, from the introduction to "*Common Sense,*" in *Thomas Paine's CollectedWritings* (NewYork,The Library of America, 1976), 5.

2. Karl Marx and Frederick Engels, *A Communist Manifesto* (New York: W.W. Norton and Company, 1988).

3. Stefan Zweig, *DieWelt von Gestern* (TheWorld ofYesterday) (Lincoln, NB: University of Nebraska Press, 1964), 412.

4. Shuichi Kato, quoting Gottfried Benn, *Kato Shuichi chosakushu* (Tokyo: Heibonsha, 1979), 203.

5. Norman Cousins, *Sekai Shimin no Taiwa* (A Dialogue Toward Global Harmonization) (Tokyo: Mainichi Press, 1991), 241.

6. Arnold Toynbee and Daisaku Ikeda, *Choose Life: A Dialogue*, ed. Richard L. Gage (New York: Oxford University Press, 1976), 318.

7. Ibid., 326.

8. *See* "Sela Sutta," *Sutta-Nipata*, trans. H. Saddhatissa (London: Curzon Press, 1987), 65.

9. Nichiren, *TheWritings of Nichiren Daishonin*, 579.

10. Ibid.

11. Ibid., 402.

12. Nichiren, *Nichiren Daishonin gosho zenshu*, 750.

13. Hans Kelsen, *What Is Justice: Justice, Law, and Politics in the Mirror of Science, Collected Essays of Hans Kelsen* (Berkeley: University of California Press, 1957), 21–22.

14. Ibid., 10.

15. Arthur Kaufmann, *Gerechtigkeit, der vergessene Weg zum Frieden:*

Gedanken eines Rechtsphilosophen zu einem politischen Thema
(München: Piper, 1986).

Chapter 7

1. Personal conversation with Gerald P. Carr.
2. U.N. Development Programme, Human Development Report,
   1996; http://www.undp.org/hdro/e96over.htm.
3. D.H. Lawrence, *Apocalypse* (London: William Heinemann Ltd.,
   1931), 104.
4. Zweig, *Die Welt von Gestern*, 329.
5. Fyodor Dostoevsky, *Complete Letters*, vol. 5, 1878–1881, ed. and
   trans. David A. Lowe (Ann Arbor: Ardis Publishers, 1991).
6. *See* Nikolai Berdjaev (1874–1948) *The Russian Idea* (New York:
   The MacMillan Company, 1948), 249.
7. Nichiren, *The Writings of Nichiren Daishonin*, 736.
8. Leo Tolstoy, *The Death of Ivan Ilyich* (New York: George Munro,
   1888), 39.
9. Nichiren, *The Writings of Nichiren Daishonin*, 279.
10. Henri Louis Bergson, *Les Deux Sources de la Morale et de la Reli-
    gion* (Paris: Librairie Felix Alcan, 1932), 30.

Chapter 8

1. Josei Toda, *Toda Josei zenshu* (The Collected Works of Josei Toda),
   vol. 4 (Tokyo: Seikyo Shimbunsha, 1984), 564–66.
2. Jonathan Schell, *The Fate of the Earth* (New York: Alfred A.
   Knopf, 1982), 119.
3. Noel Perrin, *Giving Up the Gun: Japan's Reversion to the Sword,
   1543–1879* (Boston: G.K. Hall and Company, 1979), vii.
4. Ibid., 93.
5. Ibid., 104.

6. George F. Kennan, *The Nuclear Delusion: Soviet–American Relations in the Nuclear Age* (New York: Pantheon Books, 1983), 178.

7. Special Sessions of the U.N. General Assembly on Disarmament —The author presented detailed proposals as follows: "A Ten-Point Proposal for Nuclear Disarmament" at the First Special Session, May 22, 1978; "Proposals for Disarmament and Abolition of Nuclear Weapons" at the Second Special Session, June 3, 1982; and "A Global Movement for Complete Disarmament" at the Third Special Session, June 1, 1988.

8. Kofi Annan, "The Causes of Conflict and the Promotion of Durable Peace and Sustainable Development in Africa," U.N. report, April 1998.

INDEX